711 EAU CLAIRE AVENUE

A collection of memories of growing up
in the Eau Claire district of Calgary
during the depression
and the war years.

Billy and Bobby in front of 711 Eau Claire Avenue

William M. McLennan

Fort Brisebois Publishing

"To Mom and Dad - who worked so very hard to keep a roof over our heads, to cook and sew for us, to teach us to keep our dreams realistic and not to forget that 'them that works, eats."

"To Andrew - with appreciation for the endless hours of computer work for me."

ISBN 0-9691327-6-X

Copyright, 2005, by William M. McLennan, Fort Brisebois Publishing, Calgary, Alberta. Printed by Blitzprint, Calgary, Alberta.

Mailing Address:
2108 Langriville Drive S.W.
Calgary, Alberta T3E 5G7
Canada

Contents

Do you remember 711 Eau Claire Avenue?

A two story house; kitchen attached on the back; open porch on the front. In the front yard were two tall fir trees, while along the fence was a caragana hedge. Between the two trees was a sunken wooden box; a good place to hide in. The west side of the veranda was covered with a screen of sticky vines.

Every year there was a big garden, vegetables to the front, potatoes behind. Billy and Bobby had small plots at the end.

Between the garden and the back fence was a patch of land that, for a while, held our chicken coop, rabbit pens, and where we tied up the Shetland pony. This corner of the yard was also a good place to build clubhouses, store lumber and old tires, and dig tunnels.

At the end of a long driveway was a rickety garage with a dirt floor. There was a work bench under a window at the far end, and garden tools were stacked in the corner. The garage doors were a good backstop to practise baseball pitching.

Back of the house was a tent platform, and from April until the snow came the tent was slept in. Beside the tent we built clubhouses out of the scrap lumber we were always bringing home. When the wooden back porch fell apart Bud built one of cement, but it was crumbling away too. On the porch was a wooden stand, used to stand on to hang clothes out to dry.

The cat waited until the dog got under it and would not let him out. In the cold weather the clothes on the line froze solid.

Up until the time the furnace was converted to gas, coal had to be pushed through a basement window to be stored in a basement room beneath the kitchen. This room and its adjoining crawl space had the characteristics of a dungeon.

The basement was packed full of boxes of old clothes, bottles for preserves, pails, cans, an old record player, old lamps, you name it. The furnace pipes seemed to fill half the basement. It was a very scary place in the dark. Along the side of the stairs was a ledge used to store canned goods.

The kitchen was always sunny as there were windows on the east and south sides. The wooden kitchen table sat under the east windows, while on the wide window ledge were plants, a black elephant, a clock and numerous other things. Beside the table was a wooden ice-box, but rarely was there any ice in it. The top was generally full of paper bags. Beside the back door, and under where we hung our coats, sat the washing machine, which also served as the breadbox. At first we had an old black stove, but this was later replaced with a newer model with the oven at the bottom. Cupboards lined the west wall. In a cubby hole in the corner was the sink and the hot water tank. Without a doubt this corner was a disaster.

The living room was heated by an old black stove with mica covering the front grate, so that you could see the flames of the fire dancing around inside. An upright radio sat in the corner, and after it warmed up you could listen to CJCJ. The sofa sat along the west wall, and the blind behind it was always pulled down as it looked directly on to the house next door. In the middle of the floor was a large chair that matched the sofa. Often upon one arm sat an ash tray in a miniature rubber tire. Between the hall and bedroom doors was the long side table, and on it were doilies, photos, candlesticks, and a wine coloured vase. Above the table was a painting of Castle Mountain. In the north-east corner sat the record player, and beside it and under the window was the sewing machine.

At first Marjory and Maxine slept in the living room on a Winnipeg couch. Later the blond dining room set occupied this area. There was a hanging lamp in the middle of the ceiling, while other light was provided by a floor lamp with a dark red shade.

At Christmas time there were red tinsel covered streamers hung from corner to corner in the living room. A large paper bell hung in the middle.

When we first moved to 711, Mom, Dad and Bobby slept in the big bed in the front room of the house. Billy slept on a small wooden bed minus springs. One corner of the little room had a curtain hung across it to serve as a closet. Later this was Marjory and Maxine's room.

Beside the front door and at the bottom of the stairs was a window from where a good view could be seen over the rooftops to the trees along the river. On the second floor landing sat a homemade cabinet with curtains instead of doors, a good place to keep toys and books.

The first door on the right led to the bathroom, and from its window one could have a good view south on Sixth Street to the railroad tracks. The sink was on the left, tub on the right, and in the corner a three cornered cabinet. In the top towels and hot water bottle, and down below a supply of wrappers from orange for the times that we ran out of toilet paper.

There were three bedrooms on the second floor: parents in the back bedroom, boys in the middle, and the front bedroom often rented out. This was the only room with a closet. The boys room did not have a storm window in the winter and sometimes the ice built up a half inch thick, sticking the curtains to the window in the process. The window, however, made it easy to listen to the music from the skating rink at Buffalo Stadium. Upstairs lights consisted of single bulbs at the end of long cords hanging from the ceiling. Unfortunately too often in the range of a flying pillow.

The front bedroom was the only room with a closet, and how large it seemed. From the upstairs two front windows there was a great view of the river and the North Hill.

Sometimes the house was full of people. At times there were whole groups of airmen, sometimes from Australia or England. At times our friends from the Sarcee Reserve came in their hay wagon to see us.

Every day our street was visited by the milkman and the bread man, each in their horse-pulled delivery wagon. The Chinese green-grocer and the iceman were other street sellers who used horsepower. It was only a short walk up to Fourth Avenue to catch a streetcar, and not much further to walk to town. Groceries were bought at Adam's Grocery on Fifth Street, while at the dairy on Third Avenue we bought a pitcher full of skim milk for 2 cents. Shoes went to Summerville's for repairs.

By today's standards we lacked a great deal at 711, but the old place had character and personality, leaving many pleasant memories.

Billy Loved to Run

Billy loved to run. His feet never stood still. If he wasn't running, he danced, skipped, hopped or jumped. Sometimes he ran backwards, or sideways, or in figure eight's. Sometimes he took scissor steps, or giant steps, or frog hops. Billy's legs were possessed; he never stood still, at least not for very long anyway.

Billy lived close to the river and the lovely wooded area along its banks. There were many paths through the trees. They wound in and out, going nowhere and everywhere through the trees and along the river banks. Part of the wooded area was an island, as the result of a small stream flowing out of the river, forming a pond called the mud hole, and flowing back into the river further on. What a challenge it was for Billy to jump the stream—but if the muddy banks were wet, feet slid and a wet and dirty fall resulted. But, what the heck, what is a stream if it is not to be jumped?

One day, a lovely summer day with a gentle breeze and puffy clouds floating overhead, Billy stopped at the pond, looking and listening for frogs. He waded slowly into the shallow water and the mud oozed around his black, toes-worn-out running shoes. Tadpoles wriggled and threaded their way around and through the water grass, while along the top of the water the spider-like insects scooted to and fro.

Not a sign of a frog, not even a croak. Billy trotted across the pond, water flying high and wide as his feet thrashed to break free of the sucking mud of the pond's floor.

"Ow," cried Billy as his ankle was scraped by a broken bottle sticking out of the mud. He left the by now muddy pond and trotted home to get a bandage for his wound.

"What happened now, Billy," asked his mother as she stood hanging sheets on the clothesline. "You are always running somewhere. Why can you not stay at home like your brother? He manages to amuse himself here. You would run to China if I let you."

Billy had heard this lecture before so he knew better than to argue. The cut was cleaned and , other than a sting, did not seem so bad.

"Do not leave the block; do not cross the street until your father gets home and we have supper."

"Why do we call it supper and other people call it dinner," asked Billy. His mother picked up the broom and Billy scooted out the door before she could connect.

Billy could not stand still; he practised standing long jumps in the dirt. His face lit up as he realized he could still run around the block and time himself with his Bullet pocket watch. His block, unlike most city blocks, was a perfect square - 200 feet by 200 feet - around. He knew this was true because each sidewalk block was five feet long and the block was forty squares long.

He toed the chalk line that was drawn across from the front gate, breathed deeply and, as the second hand crossed the 12, he raced away from the start. His previous best time had been about 1.02, as near as he could tell from a constantly moving watch hand. Would today be the day to beat 60 seconds?

Around the first corner, no slip and no one on the sidewalk to block his run - around Hunter's corner and on to First Avenue. The walk was clear - no girls playing hopscotch, no bikes or scooters lying across the path, no mean dogs lying in wait—the third corner was in sight!

His breathing grew heavy, his legs were weary, but he worked hard to maintain his speed, not letting any imaginary competitors pass him. Eau Clair Avenue was in sight and Billy went around Parkyn's corner fence at full stride.

Billy poured on the speed during the final stretch, but he was careful to hold his watch so that he could read his time as he crossed the finish line. He pushed hard!

As he crossed the chalk line, his glance registered less than 60 seconds. Billy slowed, gasping for breath. He looked at the watch's dial, saw the spot where he had seen the second hand at the finish line. "Holy Moses," it read 58 seconds—he finally had done it!

Just then his mother's voice came from the front porch. "Billy, get in here; you are always running somewhere just when I need you."

The 711 Ceilidh

There were times when my father, who spent so much of his time just earning a living and helping his family to survive, would invite in some friends, open up a case of beer, get out his accordion, and fill the air with music for singing and dancing. This mainly took place in the kitchen, but on a warm summer night, would flow into the back yard.

My father could not read a note of music, but he had a good ear for music and sound, and he only had to hear a piece of music or a song once and he could play it on his squeezebox.

These ceilidhs were infrequent, but very lively when they did occur.

Lesson in Economics

One job that earned me only a nickel, but was an insight into the business world, occurred when I walked into a sewing machine shop located on Sixth Avenue in the Lougheed Block. I guess they sized me up as a 'green' eight year old, and they were so right.

Anyway, I was hired to clean out an old sewing machine whose innards were full of maggots. I laboured cleaning this muck and grime for much of the morning, then went home for lunch. It was not an easy task to eat after my proximity to the maggots. I told my mother about my job, and went back to work after the usual warnings from my mother.

Upon my return to the store at one o'clock, I was handed a nickel, yes one nickel, and was told that there was not any more work.

Later, in retrospect, I realized that I had learned a lesson in pre-negotiation.

Adam's Grocery

The grocery centre to many Eau Claire families was Adam's Grocery, located on the corner of Fifth Street and First Avenue. The Adam's family lived upstairs. Many small shopkeepers of that era lived above or behind their stores.

This store was open 9 - 6, six days a week, but it was closed at one o'clock on Wednesday afternoon, a practise carried out by most Calgary stores. On that afternoon, the store's books would be taken care of, and as many families charged their groceries, there was lots of bookkeeping to do.

Some mothers would phone in an order in the morning for their son or daughter to pick up at noon on the way home from school. This seemed to me to be an important and responsible task, but because the McLennan's did not have a telephone, there was rarely anything for me to take home.

Vegetable bins were in the front, dry and canned goods on the shelf behind the counters. If they were high up, a clamp on the end of a stick brought them down for the grocer.

Mr. Adams was very good at paying you two cents for the return of a pop bottle, although most grocers located further south expected you to take the refund in candy.

Adam's store had a wide front porch where kids could sit to drink their pop, eat their candy, and watch the world go by.

Adult Clubs in the Eau Claire

Being curious and nosey, we kids were always mystified as to who went to where and what went on at the various adult clubs located in the Eau Claire area.

The Army and Navy Veterans of Canada occupied a large lovely house and grounds located on Fourth Avenue, east of Third Street. There was always someone at the front door who requested us to leave the yard, however we could stand at the back fence to watch the lawn bowling and see the garden parties.

In Chinatown, which edged Eau Claire, there was the Dart Coon Club, Chinese Club, Lee's Association and the YMCA Chinese Mission. In the back of several Chinese stores on Centre Street, we, by peeking through doorways, could watch the very heated and noisy card and table games.

The Central Community Club was located in a building on the east end of Eau Claire Avenue. However the closest had a face with a severe expression peering out the window.

Air Raid Precautions

In September of 1939 war was declared on Germany. "Extra, Extra, read all about it, Canada at war," shouted the newsboys as they worked their way down to Eau Claire Avenue, selling their special editions of the Herald. This was a scary happening for little children, let alone adults.

Calgary was put on alert for possible bombings. Air raid wardens were appointed and directions given for blackouts and fire protection. All windows had to be covered so that, if needed, not a sliver of light would show through. In addition each household was to have a pail of sand handy in the event of an incendiary bomb landing.

On test nights, when practise conditions were in effect, Mr. Mobray, our local air-raid warden, dressed with his helmet and official arm band, made the rounds of the houses in the neighborhood to make certain that all of the imposed conditions were met.

Airplane Battles

Airplane battles were best played with four players, two as the British and two as the Germans. Naturally we all wanted to be a British pilot, but fairness prevailed and we interchanged roles.

Where did we get the airplanes? Why just by extending our arms as wings and with motor and gun noise created by our mouths.

"Zoom, roar, rat-a-tat, bang, your on fire; got you, got you, your on fire, I shot out your motor; I shot you, you were under me, you were not aimed at me; Jimmy got you when you were after me; your hit, you must crash."

Sometimes we did crash, not on the ground, but into each other. Winding and turning, while on the dead run we would crash into each other, then an argument would ensue as to who was to blame.

Sometimes we would play the same game, but we used model airplanes held by two fingers, letting them do manoeuvres above our heads.

So often while we were acting out these aerial battles there were the R.C.A.F. training planes flying overhead.

Airplanes

After my father had watched me, with arms outstretched, imitating the manoeuvres of the airplane over Calgary, he told me that he would take me to the airport. The next day, being Sunday, he loaded us into the car, and then drove us over the Langevin Bridge and up to the Renfrew Airport. Here there were several two wing planes tied down and in the curved roof hanger, were two more planes.

The planes all had two wings, large propellers in front of the engine and two spaces for the pilot and a passenger. Although I had seen these planes flying over Eau Claire and doing daring manoeuvres in the sky, I had no idea as to how they were able to take off from the ground.

From the distance was the drone of an orange coloured plane, but with just one wing on the top, which came into view and landed, bouncing along the ground. I learned that this plane was a Curtis Robin, and for a dollar and a half, you could have a 15 minute plane ride to view the city. I turned to my father, but he said, "A dollar and a half would feed you for a week."

Later, other pilots, wearing leather jackets and aviator's hats, with long side straps and goggles, came out of the hanger and went to their planes. Other men lifted the plane's tails to turn them around, and then cranked the propeller to start the engines.

The planes went down the field gathering speed and then took off into the air where they did maneuvers,

I went home with 'plane fever'. We made crude airplanes out of wood pieces. Propellers were cut from cardboard and attached with a shingle nail. We held our own maneuvers flying loop the loops. The next Christmas I was pleased to find my own kid's aviator helmet under the tree.

April Fool's Day

April Fool's Day was a special day for most of the people in the Eau Claire who worked long and hard just to put food on the table. Here was one day when silliness could be accepted.

Most jokes were of a verbal nature that were played on family or friends. If there was a time for teasing, this was it, although many families had a common sense rule of not teasing your little brother or sister. It was a good time to get back at your big sisters or your parents. However, we sometimes forgot that they were wiser than us.

On March 30, I had a brilliant plan or switching salt for sugar in the pressed glass sugar bowl. I did this when no one was looking before I went to bed.

The next morning my mother called me to get up and come down to eat my oatmeal porridge while it was still hot. There was something scary in the sound of her voice. I started to nibble at the oatmeal and then her words were, "Put some sugar on it." I could not do it knowing it was salt and how I hated the taste of salt. Mom took a spoonful, put it on my porridge and said, "You are not moving from that chair until it is all eaten up."

I fussed and whined, finally apologizing for my inconsiderate and wasteful joke. Mom was true to her word and her belt, and I had to sit there until the cold and bitter porridge was at least half eaten. She then gave me a warm hug and said, "Sometimes jokes backfire."

The Army Huts

Not long after war was declared in 1939, a group of army barracks were constructed on the vacant land north of the armoury. These buildings served as a staging place for the new recruits. Each long wooden building contained two rows of metal bunks, and there were simple washrooms at each end of the building. A central mess hall served all of the facilities.

It was the mess hall that several of 'us' kids used to go to. We were generally welcomed and often fed copious amounts of bacon and bread. The dishes were heavy; white bowls, cups and plates. Sometimes we would earn our food by sweeping the dining room floor.

Following the end of the war, the huts were moved or pulled down. However the recreation hut, a little wider and higher in size, located close to the banks of the river, was left in place. It served as the home of Calgary's Senior Basketball League for several seasons.

Aviation

Many of the Eau Claire boys gazed in awe at the sky when the twin-winged aeroplanes flew over the city, often doing stunts, including the most dangerous 'Loop-the-Loop' The air maneuvers kindled the desire in many of us to become a pilot and fly high over the city.

One day my sister told me of the Jimmy Allen club for boys and girls who were keen on aeroplanes. I asked my sister to take me to join in order to get my membership card and my wings.

Finally, she took me to the B.A. service station on Fourth Street near Knox Church. Outside was a large sign that read "Boys and girls, join the Jimmy Allen Club." On the sign was a picture of Jimmy Allen wearing his flying Helmut.

We went into the office where I was given a list of the club's rules, a membership card and a 'real' propeller pin to wear on my sweater. This was the first club I had ever belonged to.

After war was declared, several air force bases were opened around Calgary. The sky was full of aeroplanes each day, training pilots for the war.

Baking Bread

"I am baking bread tomorrow, Billy. Would you like to grease the pans?"

I replied, "Indeed, Mom, I would be happy to grease the pans."

Mom mixed up the dough and added the yeast to make the bread rise. It was all very magical to me as to how a small cake of yeast could make the dough swell up so much. I greased the pans with the paper that the butter was wrapped with.

Mom put the dough loaves in the pans and covered them with a clean dishcloth that had been made out of a flour sack. Then the oven was warmed up and the pans placed in it. You could smell the stove's heat, then after a while, the lovely smell of baking bread began to fill the kitchen.

The big black stove was heated by gas, and with the oven, there was very little control over the temperature. It was either on or off. Mom checked the bread and finally pulled the pans out and the bread began to cool. What a wonderful smell, but the bread had to cool further before Mom would cut it. She then added butter and jam and gave me two delicious slices.

Balancing

The ability to balance was very high in the values of the kids of Eau Claire. If you were at the railroad tracks it was to stand on a rail, one foot in front of another and arms wide to help maintain balance. To slip off meant a fall to the depths below. We practised so much that we could walk the rail backwards or even run along a track. Sometimes we would put an ear to the rail to hear if there was a train coming.

Walking the tops of fences also provided lots of balancing practise. This could prove dangerous though as pant bottoms could catch on a picket or a loose wire, or your weight could cause the fence to sag and down you might tumble. A front door might open and the homeowner would yell at you to get off the fence.

Around the boy's east playground at McDougall School, was a fence made of parallel pipes imbedded in cement posts. Walking these pipes was, to a small boy, comparable to walking a high tight rope.

Bananas for Dessert

The Scott National Company was located on Ninth Avenue between Second and Third Streets West. A spur railway line ran down the alley and freight cars were dropped there to allow the fruit and produce to be unloaded. Stalks of bananas were hung from hooks or piled unwrapped in the cars, and as a result, many bananas came loose from the stalk.

Along came the boys from Eau Claire with their canvas Albertan bags. With the consent of the foreman or the labouring men, the bags were filled with loose, overripe or bruised bananas.

We staggered from the weight of the bananas towards home, sometimes selling three bananas for a nickel. If we ran into a hobo, we would give him one or two. After we ate a banana the skin would be spread on the sidewalk with the optimism that a comic-strip type fall by some unsuspecting pedestrian would occur, but I doubt that it ever happened.

On arriving home mom would nag about us being by the railroad tracks; however, the bananas were always welcome.

The Band

Some of the Eau Claire kids came to 711 to be part of the band. We had found that dinner knives, if held correctly, would vibrate and serve very well as drumsticks on dinner plates or jam tins. We had cigar box banjos, mouth organs, tin horns, whistles, Jews' harp and bells. Sometimes, but only sometimes, my father would let me use his accordion, otherwise known as a squeezebox.

There were only a few tunes or songs that we all knew. There was always someone who could not keep time, or sang too loud, or out of tune. It was very difficult to be a good conductor and please everybody. Our practises were not long, because, after the dog started to howl, Mom would come out and send everyone home.

Barns, Sheds and Coops

Did you ever walk by a barn and smell the hay in the loft? Hay has a pleasant smell. The dairy stable on First Avenue provided this to the people of Eau Claire. The sawmill also had a barn for its horses. There were other buildings in the district that had been used as barns way, way back in the 'old days'. Some had been improved on and were now used as dwellings. Some were now used as garages, and sometimes the children of the house had a play area in the loft.

Most every yard had a shed or two. Garden tools, bicycles and snow shovels found storage there.

There were numerous coops or pens, often attached to a shed or garage. Yes, chickens were kept there, and roosters could be heard early in the morning.

Another type of coop, sometimes on the ground, sometimes on stilts, or sometimes on a roof, was used for pigeons. There were lots of pigeons in the Eau Claire. They would flock, landing on the rooftops, and their cooing sounds filled the air. Sometimes you could see a cat, sitting on a rooftop, watching the pigeons.

Many yards had huts, built by the children, for the children. As many Eau Claire houses were small and families large, a place to call your own, no matter how modest, was welcome.

Baseball

Baseball was a large part of many an Eau Claire boy's summer, including mine.

The first glove I used was just an old leather glove borrowed from my mother. It was hardly enough, but it did stop some of the sting. By about age ten I managed to buy a second hand glove, but there was one small problem - I was left-handed and it was for a right-handed person. What a difference, I could now actually catch the odd fly.

Many an hour I spent by myself in the dirt driveway, pitching towards the cross boards on the garage doors. The heavy lacrosse ball I used would bounce back to me if I hit the garage door straight on, but if I hit the edge of the cross boards the ball would fly out into the garden or bounce off of the house.

Finally, at the age of thirteen, I was able to find a left-handed glove at McFarlane and Wilson Sporting Goods, located on Eighth Avenue. The uniqueness of the new glove was that it had three fingers instead of five.

I slept with that glove, spit on it, oiled it, pounded it to form a pocket and learned respect for personal property that would affect my future values. There were times that, next to your dog, your baseball glove was your best friend.

A Baseball Game

"Baseball game today, Billy; see you at the school diamond."

I loved to play baseball, but I wasn't very good against the bigger boys. I found the old leather glove that had been my mother's, but something was better than nothing, and it sure helped to cut down the sting of stopping a line drive.

When I arrived at the McDougall diamond there were a few fellows there, just playing catch with the one baseball available. Some players had baseball gloves, some had a winter glove, and others just had bare hands.

Finally, someone said, "Let's pick teams; Dee and Chuck are captains. To determine who got first pick, the captains marched their hand along the bat until only Chuck would touch the end, so he got to choose first. I counted the players, a total of fourteen, so at least I would get to play.

Chuck and Dee stood apart, in turn naming their choice of players, with the best and biggest going first.

Finally, there was only Pee-wee and myself left. "Oh, please God, don't let me be picked last again." Chuck looked at both of us, someone giggled, then a single word, "Billy." Pee-wee was last, not me, to be picked.

They put me in the field, but I did well there because I like to run, stop the grounders with my shins and hurl the ball back to the infielders.

I was the last to bat, but Dee lobbed a slow one, and while my eyes were closed, drove the ball over third base and I ran for first. Stealing bases was easy. I took a lead off from third, stole home when the catcher chased a bad pitch, and I scored our team's first run!

Sandlot league Tigers at Mewata ball park

Tigers Sandlot League Finalists, 1945
Gillis, Yonden, Loft, McLennan, Clark, Kolber, Gobel, Petley
Steel, Therialt, B. Boon, Grover, W. Boon

Bed Linen

Bed linen at 711 Eau Claire Avenue was of a great variety and quality. I know I often slept on a patterned pillowcase, but not one of a flower design, but one that had Robin Hood Flour stamped on it. Not soft cotton, but a good one to keep the feather ends from coming through to scratch your face. If one leaned out the window and looked to the south, it was possible to see the towers of the Robin Hood Mills, which were located on Ninth Avenue and Fourth Street, South West, one of the largest structures in the downtown. Robin Hood, as well as other flour sacks, were often used as pillowcases or used to make clothing for many Calgary and Prairie people.

Sheets were often hand-me-downs from my parents or my sister's beds. Thin, yes, raggedy, yes, with holes, yes, patched, yes. It was not a good idea to put a sheet with a hole on it on my bed because, as a habit of little boys, their toes would find it and the hole would gather longer and wider and bigger.

Our middle bedroom was not very warm, as little heat made its way up through the register from the furnace in the basement. This coal furnace had been converted to natural gas, but only because hot air rose did it function, as there was not any fan to assist it. There was not any storm pane on the window and we kept it open to hear the music from the skating rink at Buffalo Stadium. Ice formed quickly on the window glass, the window frame, and if it got really cold on the wall alongside the window.

This meant lots of blankets, heavy, itchy, grey woolen blankets, patch work quilts that had been made from a hundred and one different pieces of discarded cloth stuffed with various cotton and wool fleeces.

From May through October, we slept in a white canvas tent that was erected on a wooden platform in the backyard. In the heat of the summer, the sides could be rolled up. An old iron bed crossed the backside of the tent and two Winnipeg couches were placed along the sides. There was not a coil spring as part of any of the three beds.

Naturally, sleeping outside you had the cat in your bed, then the dog walking several turns around before settling down heavy on your legs.

Early in the morning, there was the crow of the rooster and the clucking of the hens, plus a heavy bladder with it being a long ways to the bathroom on the second floor of the house.

There were mornings in the fall when you would awaken to find the tents surface just a few inches above your face, compressed from a heavy, quiet fall of snow during the night.

It was always a challenge to last another night, and then another in the tent as winter slowly took over from fall. However, to again sleep upstairs in the middle bedroom, bathroom down the hall, electric light and the warmth of the house was always welcome.

Big Business

After my success with selling lemonade at the laundry, I decided that there was a greater retailing challenge by selling uptown. So I put an apple box on my old red wagon, used some crayons to make a sign on a piece of cardboard, made two quart bottles of lemonade and set off for Eighth Avenue.

It was hot and the wagon was heavy. The lemonade slopped over the top of the bottles that I had wedged into the box with pieces of cardboard. I could see that the only thing to do was to drink a little from each bottle. Finally, I arrived on the south side of Eaton's, where there was some shade provided by the awnings. A few people walked by, some smiled and an old lady giggled, but nobody was buying. Finally, a well-dressed man, wearing a straw hat, stopped by and asked how business was.

I told him that sales were not so good. Anyway, he patted me on the shoulder, put a quarter in my hand and said, "Never quit trying."

Needless to say, sales were not good, the lemonade got warmer and I got thirstier. I took a long drink and started home. By Fourth Avenue, I was hot and tired, but another cupful helped the journey and the disappointment of not so good sales.

When Mom asked about the success of my venture, I showed her the quarter and told her about my newly learned advice.... "Never quit trying."

Birds and Animals

We grew up with lots of pets at 711 Eau Claire Avenue.

We were awakened each morning by the chirping and singing of Mom's canary. Much of the time, I had the task of filling the water dish and seed bowl.

Our only cat was Tiny, small and multi coloured, that my brother had brought home. Tiny had numerous litters of kittens, but sad as it may seem, my father would put them in a gunnysack and drown them in the river, a common practise in those days.

We always had a dog or two. Pal, a Shepherd crossbreed, was my best friend and companion for many years. Then we got Sport, a German Shepherd, to guard the house. One day my father brought home a British Bulldog, whose jaw was shaped in such a way that it could hardly pick up food.

A part of our family, and the neighbourhood pet, was Teddy, my Shetland pony. Teddy was ridden almost everywhere a small boy went, including to McDougall School, but the principal soon put a stop to that.

We had rabbits, pigeons, a pen full of chickens and a rooster to wake us up in the morning. We had goldfish, turtles and a salamander that was found in the yard. It seems that the rabbit pen almost always had some occupants. Much to the disgust of my mother, there were times when we had a box of mice from the basement.

One Saturday morning my father left early and came back while my mother was still in bed. He marched up the stairs and into their bedroom with a young lion on a leash. This was the R.C.A.F. station's mascot, and it brought screams from my mother.

The neighbourhood was full of free running dogs, cats howling at night, fish, frogs, beaver and muskrats in the river, flocks of birds, pigeons and there were the tradesmen's horses. Periodically the dogcatcher paid a visit to Eau Claire Avenue.

The Black Maria

The Calgary Police force was composed mainly of foot constables, who walked the Calgary streets. Each constable had his own beat or district, but there were call boxes placed on telephone poles. The chief had an automobile, and there were some mounted constables.

If there was a need to transport someone or to retrieve a stolen or lost bicycle then the Black Maria was brought into use. This black van brought fear and excitement if it pulled onto Eau Claire Avenue. Was it for a body in the river, a hobo who had overstepped the bounds of propriety, or because a Mrs. had taken a rolling pin to her wayward or lazy husband? Perhaps because most of the Eau Claire Kids had a guilty conscience we could be afraid and wary.

Blood Brothers

There was a mystic club among some of the older boys in Eau Claire. It was a private organization and membership was by invitation only. There was lots of talk and gossip about this club, but no one really seemed to know who was in it.

When I attempted to talk to my Mom about this club, she warned me not to try anything like that ourselves. That even brought about a stronger desire to imitate the secret ritual of joining such a club.

What was the secret rite that my mother told me not to even talk about? It seemed that you had to take a knife, cut your finger and mix your blood with the other club members to become blood brothers. Did it really work?

Bottle Cap Shoe Scrapper

There were those households in Eau Claire where the shoe cleaning boards, placed outside the door, were made from bottle caps that were nailed bottom side up to a board with shingle nails.

Big Orange, Big Lemon, Coca-Cola, Seven-Up, Stubby, Pepsi, Root Beer, Orange Crush, Big Lime, Calgary Brewing, Lethbridge Brewing, all sorts of bottle caps. Why bottle caps; well, the corrugated edges were sharp and did well to help remove the dirt and mud from the soles of boots and shoes.

The Boxing Gym

One day I was invited by some Eau Claire kids to go to the boxing gym. My Mom said it was okay with her, but "Do not come home with a bloody nose."

The gym was up the stairs to a second floor of a building just east of the Strand Theatre, and was owned by Ernie Farr. Here was the first boxing ring that I had ever seen, let alone been in a gym. Besides the ring, there were punching bags, weights, wall mirrors and boxing posters.

Ernie liked to work with boys and teenagers, perhaps hoping to discover and develop a potential champion. He showed us how the gloves should be tied on, stance, footwork, jabs and how to cover up. Then two of the Eau Claire boys, who had been there before, got into the ring for a round of boxing. Their footwork was great, but they seemed afraid of 'mixing-it-up'

Boxing looked easy, so I volunteered to get into the ring next. The gloves were tied on me and I looked forward to utilizing my speed and strength. The bell went and then I realized that my defensive skills were zero as I was punched on the shoulders, chest, arms and head. I found myself turning away from the punches and retreating backwards. Clearly, my opponent's skills had me on the run, and it seemed like eternity before the bell sounded, and I, beaten and embarrassed, got my glove off.

When I got home Mom asked, "Did you get a bloody nose?"

I replied, "I couldn't be caught."

Brask

"If a job is worth doing, it's worth doing well"

We had an old, oil-smelling garage at 711. There was a workbench under the south window, a dirt floor and lots of old lumber and garden tools in the corner. My father would often gather there with some of his friends to work on a project, or just to talk and have a smoke.

One of my father's friends was Brask, who was born in Denmark and talked with a strong accent.

One day I was working on a small boat, which was a flat piece of wood, a couple of thread spools nailed on and an attempt of a sail. I had used phonograph needles in place of small nails. I had done this work in my usual sloppy manner and Brask politely pointed out how to improve it. Probably my attitude suggested that it really did not matter.

Brask replied, "If a job is worth doing, its worth doing well." These words were to be imprinted on my mind.

Breakfast, Dinner and Supper

As with many children the food our mothers prepared and fathers worked hard to provide, could be taken for granted.

With an old gas stove and an icebox that rarely held ice, Mom's work was not easy. Most of the time she made porridge for breakfast. Robin Hood Rolled Oats, Sunnyboy, Red River Cereal were what she cooked, sometimes our choice, sometimes hers. Sometimes Mom threw some raisins into the porridge pot. On special occasions, we were allowed Corn Flakes or Muffets.

Juice was a rare drink, and it just might consist of oranges that she had squeezed.

Mom made toast over the gas flame, and more often than not it was partially burned. Sometimes a fried or poached egg and most often cocoa, hopefully without a curd skin floating on the top.

Our noon meal was called dinner. When you heard the whistle from the sawmill or the laundry you had better be home fast. Mom usually served soup, sandwiches, milk and a cookie.

Supper, was served when my father arrived home, not long after five. The dog often licked off my plate, and my sisters washed the supper dishes at the old cracked sink in the corner.

Almost always, my fourth meal, after pyjamas were on and just prior to bed, was bread and jam, peanut butter or sugar and cocoa.

A belated thank you to Mom for preparing so much with so few resources,

Brown Bobbys

There were many people in the Eau Claire that lived a hand-to-mouth existence, and I suppose, at times, we did too.

Across the alley, although it wasn't really an alley but a narrow field, was a very small house. The low attic had been made into a bedroom where two of the boys entered by way of a ladder and slept. This was the home of the Joiner family, Mom, Dad and a half dozen kids.

Times were tough, jobs were not easy to find, but this family had its own business, such as it was. They made and sold "Brown Bobbys' . This was a triangular shaped donut, cut from dough, made in their kitchen and then cooked in a special oil in a small machine in their enclosed front porch. Production was not large, but the meagre sales of Brown Bobbys helped to put food on the family's table. I know what they had for dessert.

Brush Your Teeth Billy

The brush was worn, but it was mine. The unpleasant part was dipping it into the jar of baking soda and then scrubbing. Without fail the solution would get behind my teeth and then I felt that horrible taste as the soda touched the taste buds. If I knew then what I experienced later in life I would have scrubbed twice as hard and twice as often.

Buffalo Stadium

Buffalo Stadium was located between Fifth and Sixth Streets, north of First Avenue.

In earlier days this had been the location of the Eau Claire sawmill log pound. A channel connected this body of water with the river, and logs were stored here until they could be cut.

By the 1930's the log pound had been filled in, but the channel and the river's wear and tear created a circuitous stream that created an island and some delicate areas where the fish laid many eggs and the minnows abounded.

Along what would be Eau Claire Avenue the city had installed swings and a slide, teeter-totters and a merry-go-round. On the south-west corner of this block was a small building, which housed the Calgary Casket Factory. We had our doubts as to whether this building was haunted, but never the less we probably crossed to the other side of the street and ran a little faster when we passed it in the dark.

Later it became a puffed wheat factory. You could take a pillowcase over, and for ten cents, they would fill it full of delicious puffed wheat.

In the winter, the city would put up boards and flood a rink adjacent to First Avenue. We would often pasture Teddy, our horse, in the alfalfa patch north of the factory.

Back to Buffalo Stadium; at the start of the war, the naval recruits leveled off a marching and drill area, which was used until their new indoor facilities on Seventh Avenue and Third Street West, were ready.

About 1942 the Calgary Brewing and Malting came in possession of the block and constructed the ballpark.

Home base was located in the northeast corner. The left and right foul lines were less than three hundred feet. Right field had a distinct jag in the fence as it was constructed around the factory. Centre field had almost a right angle, with a depth of over 400 feet.

The eight-foot high fence was completely covered with eight by ten foot painted panels advertising local commercial and industrial firms. This was an art form in its own right and the fans often discussed the merits of such.

A scoreboard, entered by a wall ladder, was perched above the centrefield fence, and it made use of a local girl to post the inning-by-inning score.

Bleachers rose high behind home plate, and then they were progressively lower as they extended along both sides. A press box topped the section directly behind home plate.

As the crowds increased, the bleachers along the first base line were extended right to the left field fence. On popular weekend games, the spectators lined the entire outfield fence. A ball hit among them counted as a double.

The two entrance gates were located in the southeast corner. On the east side was the clubhouse, dressing rooms and concession building. A smaller building housed the seat cushions, which were rented out for 10 cents each.

During the war years, there were baseball teams from the navy, the army, two air force teams, the Yanks, and two civilian teams, The Detroit (auto body) Bears and Purity 99. Sometimes teams from the air bases at Great Falls, Montana, Alaska or Edmonton played at Buffalo Stadium.

Visiting U S Air Force Baseball team

Pitcher John Carpenter — won 18, lost 2

Buffalo Stadium from center field

Harry Ornest - second base, future owner of the St. Louis Blues Hockey Team

Cadets

Many Eau Claire boys belonged to a cadet core. There were sea cadets, air cadets, army cadets and high school groups.

In theory, you were supposed to be twelve years old and be able to meet the minimum height regulation. Being a very small kid, this was a problem, and, as well, I was a year short from age twelve. Part of the size regulation was uniforms had to reasonably fit, and to get a uniform was perhaps the main reason for joining the cadets.

Twice my joining was turned down because I did not meet the height. However, with a little growth, my curly hair combed high, and best of all, thick inserts of cardboard in the heels of my boots. My height was now, just barely, the necessary measurement.

Mom turned up the pant legs and shortened the sleeves. The uniform still hung on me, but then I would be growing, hopefully. Boots were polished and buttons shined. I had to learn to tie the necktie and to adjust my hat to just the right angle. How proud I was when everything fitted together.

Friday night cadets were held in the old fire hall across from Victoria Park. Besides marching and rifle drill there were classes, sports and band practise. The cadets had a bugle and drum band, and I learned to play the bugle.

After cadets, many of us would go to the local café for a bottle of Big Orange or Big Lemon.

Army cadet camp at Sylvan Lake

Calendars

Late each fall I, usually by myself, would visit stores and businesses in the area to gather calendars. There was always room in our house for a few calendars. Sometimes the pictures were so pleasant that Mom just cut the calendar part off and left the picture to decorate the wall.

There were some stores and firms that you had learned not to go to because you would be curtly told, "No!" There were other places where you would be put on trial and questioned, and you still might not get a calendar.

The best approach was to ask to see their calendar, admire it and compliment the picture and text. Flattery, yes, but it was the best approach. Sometimes the owner was not in and an employee could be persuaded to part with the picture. Sometimes banks would have them sitting on the counter, but often they did not have a picture. Perhaps the best calendars were those put out by the Hudson's Bay Company, but to come into possession of one was a challenge in itself.

Calling Children Home

Eau Claire was full of many children of all ages. Groups and gangs evolved. Friendships and interests came and went. Whatever activity that was current and what kids were part of made it the centre of the universe.

However, these activities could be generally brought to a halt as mothers came out to their porch or front gate to call their offspring home. There were those parents who used a whistle, sometimes carved from wood by the father. The whistle's noise would be distinctive and carry a long way. Woe to the child who did not scurry home at its sound.

Younger children would be called home first. Sometimes, the message was to an older child to send of bring the younger sibling home.

There were those mothers who called their child's name, then followed this with a sound, either simple or a yodel, or a soft sound and the tail end of the name as a thrill or a screech.

Later, there would be second calls, often followed by a threat. This could be followed by the father; loud, gruff and threatening.

There were those mothers whose voices were imitated by some of the kids. If Tommy were called, his friends would imitate her voice, much to the distress of Tommy.

There were those mothers who stood at the front gate holding their broom, and if she were to come looking for her child, the broom might just be used.

Sometimes, while I was hidden behind a garage or fence, pretending that I had not heard my father, he would send Sport, our dog, to smell us out, and when he did, he would grab my sleeve in his teeth to pull me home.

If we were down at the river, especially on the ice and out of range, we knew that whoever came looking most often carried a stick or belt. Then it was a race to get home first, get pyjamas on and into bed.

Car Repair Pits

Not that many families in Eau Claire owned an automobile. However, with winter conditions being what they were, car owners most often went to the extra effort of keeping the vehicle under cover.

Older barns were utilized and, as well, there were numerous small garages. Many of these structures were unique because in the middle was a pit about four feet deep in the dirt. There would be wooden steps at one end to enter it. What was the purpose of these pits? They were used as a means to get under the car to service and repair it.

How automobiles worked was a mystery to many young Eau Claire boys. By going down into these pits while a car sat overhead gave us some insight into the 'horseless carriage'

Catalogues

The most popular books for many in Eau Claire, and elsewhere, were the T. Eaton and Hudson's Bay catalogues. Where else, other than the stores themselves, could a person feast their eyes on such a grand array of goods, be it clothing, household goods, sporting goods, tools and toys.

There was great anticipation prior to the arrival of the catalogues, and in many households, there was a pecking order in who got to read through them. Family members would often make a pencil notation on those goods that they may want for Christmas or a birthday.

Older catalogues were often left in the bathroom or outhouse to provide reading material for a few minutes of relaxation. The catalogues were excellent aids in teaching reading and research skills.

Catching Pigeons

One day at school, my friend Cyril invited me to catch pigeons under Centre Street Bridge. Cyril was by far the smartest kid at McDougall School so I would often go along with what he had planned. His mother ran a butter and egg stall in the City Hall Market, so he had lots of time of his own.

I met him at the bridge that evening. He had a flashlight and a net made of gunny sacking on the end of a pole. I could hear the pigeons cooing as we climbed out onto the arches, and there were the pigeons. Cyril turned on the flashlight and slowly moved closer to the pigeons. He shone the flashlight into their eyes, and slowly bringing the net around, he dropped it over two birds. The rest quickly flew to another arch.

We took the sack with the two frightened pigeons in it to a store in Chinatown. They knew Cyril and paid him ten cents for each of the two pigeons. It was getting dark and I was seven blocks from home, so I ran all the way.

Catching Sucker Fish

"Billy, Billy, the rivers down. Let's go catch some sucker fish and sell them - hurry!"

From the kitchen came the sound of my mother's voice, "Don't you leave this yard until your work is done." Pleading did not help, but it did hold me up for five minutes when the work could have been finished in two minutes, such is a child's logic or lack of.

We hurried to the river and saw that the flow was very low; the result of some dam that we knew was near the mountains, but which we had never seen. Shoes came off and we waded across the log channel to the weir made out of huge timbers that joined Princess Island to the narrow island that stretched to Louise Bridge. Under the weir, which had also served as a bridge, were several dark and quiet pools, which, if you stirred up the muddy bottom, would hide the suckers that gathered there. The smell of this water was dank and there was a sinister feeling in this spot, so close to the beauty of the river, but never touched by the sunlight.

In the deepest pool floated a school of suckers, almost blending with the muddy bottom. Thoughts of quicksand was in our minds as we stepped into the mud, which sucked out bare feet in. While one of us stood still, the other moved and directed the suckers to within reach of a hand that was held motionless under water, and attempts were made to grab a fish. Finally, one of these ugly creatures was caught and put in the tin lard pail that we had brought. The water was now too muddy for further attempts.

We waded back across the log channel to where we had left our black running shoes, a style that was to make a fashion comeback years later.

After going home for a jam sandwich and another lecture from Mom, we took our catch and headed down to Chinatown to sell it. We would barter for what seemed forever to get a dime rather than a nickel for this creature from the muddy deep. Most often, we had to settle for the coin with the beaver on it.

Whether these fish were for home consumption, or were added to a menu of a café, we never did know.

Catching Suckers

At the west end of Prince's Island, about 6A Street, was a weir with a narrow bridge over the top to connect the main island with the narrow island that extended to Louise Bridge to create the log channel. High waters flowed back to the main channel through the weir.

There were times when the flow of water in the Box was curtailed by a dam further upstream. When this happened, it made pools of water under the bridge and the weir accessible to little boys who would take the opportunity to catch the big, slow, suckerfish that bottom fed in the mud of the pools.

We soon learned that wading into the pools mudded the water and we could not see the fish. Crude nets were made of old wire screen tied in a funnel shape and nailed on a long stick. Preserve bottles, pails with holes in them, and gunnysack nets were all tried, but with limited success.

Although the suckers were slow swimmers it still took a bit of luck to catch one, and on a rare day, two. Catching one of these creatures was only the first step in the due process. We had to keep them alive in a bucket until we reached our sales destination.

It was a long walk to the Chinese cafes on Centre Street, so we would put the pail containing the sucker in the back of an old wagon, hoping that the wheels would stay on. At the first café, we would negotiate for ten cents, but being offered only five cents in flip-flop English. Of course, our speech ended up somewhat the same. Usually we ended up settling for a nickel, which would often be spent in the grocery store next door for ginger.

Cellophane

If your father smoked, there were always pieces of cellophane available that had been wrapped around the tobacco products. This material was so thin, so clear, so flexible and so mysterious as to how it could be manufactured. If you made a shoebox miniature house, it could be put over the windows to imitate glass.

There was another use for cellophane, a use that gave you lots of giggles and shivers. If you took a piece of cellophane, stretched it tight, placed it close to your lips and gently blew on it, then the effects sent shivers through your lips and pressed your giggle button. Was it fun, yes! Did it do any harm, I doubt it,

Chinese Market Gardeners

There were several Chinese vegetable and fruit peddlers that made the rounds in the Eau Claire. Their produce wagons, each pulled by one horse, were the most dilapidated of the various company wagons, and whose squeaky wheels preceded their arrival.

Many mothers preferred to go out to the wagon to view the quality and quantity of the fruit and vegetables. For others, the Chinese seller would carry a wicker basket with a variety of produce to the kitchen door.

A balance scale hung in the back of the van to be used to weigh the goods. A hand held abacus helped with the mathematics of selling.

Some Eau Claire boys teased the market gardeners, taunting them or putting a stick through the spokes of a wheel to stop its movement.

We knew so little about these fruit sellers, where were they from, where did they live, did they have boys like us at home?

Christmas Parties and Concerts

Prior to Christmas many clubs and other organizations held Christmas concerts and parties for the children of members. Few of the children in the Eau Claire had parents who were in the same social or business circles as to be part of these events.

Nevertheless, dates and places of these functions became general knowledge among the less fortunate children in the area, It was reported that on occasions, such as often, certain children would attend some of these functions to feast on pop and cake. After the children's names had been called and presents handed out the uninvited guests would approach the Christmas tree, and the now tired 'hander-outer' of the goods to state their name had not been called and that they did not receive a present.

Often the person would reach under the tree to pick out an unclaimed book or puzzle for these 'street children.

A Christmas Present from Scotland

One day at noon, after running home from McDougall School, I was surprised to see a huge parcel addressed to Master William McLennan, wrapped in brown paper, tied with twine and numerous British stamps, some of which I had never seen before.

"Can I open it Mom?"

"No, Billy, eat your soup and bread; we can open it later when your father gets home."

I went back to school and told my friends about this wondrous package that I had received from my grandparents in Scotland. "Oh Billy, it's just a lump of coal," said Robin, who was familiar with Scottish customs.

After school, instead of hanging around to 'kick the ball' I hurried home to hold and squeeze the package. It did not feel like a lump of coal to me.

Finally, after supper, my father cut the twine and allowed me to unwrap the parcel. My eyes grew wide as a tartan kilt, a jacket with shiny silver buttons and a tam with a Gordon Highlander badge came into view. Now I was a true Scot, and I wore the tam for years.

No lump of coal though.

Christmas was Coming

Planning for Christmas started at school where the students spent their art periods designing and drawing Christmas cards for our parents and relatives. Very simple decorations for the tree were made from red or green paper. Snow flakes made by folding paper and then cutting out angels of paper, produced designs of snowflakes and filled the maker full or awe.

Sometime in early December, our friends, the Sarcees, would arrive in Eau Claire with a hay wagon loaded with Christmas trees that they had cut on the reserve. The service station on Fourth Avenue sold Christmas trees, but they were much more expensive than Starlight's prices.

My father would make a wooden stand, which was nailed to the bottom of the tree, which was then placed beside the window in our living room. This was beside the Winnipeg couch where my sisters slept.

Red streamers were strung from corner to corner across the living room. In the middle of the room was hung a large paper bell that magically could be opened from a flat bell to a round one.

Hanging in the window was my favourite decoration, a red wreath with a candle and ribbon in the middle.

We had a string of eight lights on the tree, but if one light went out they would all go out. Strings of red and green paper were wound around the tree. We had a few magical glass balls, made in far off Nippon. The cat liked to bat them. There were paper decorations that we had made at school. The pride and joy of seeing your own work on the tree filled you with a sense of accomplishment.

The angel decoration at the top of the tree was made of a toilet paper tube, wings of cardboard, a hand painted face and a dress of bits of lace.

The cat loved the tree and its decorations for here was a place to hide and many things to smell, pull and bat at.

Climbing Trees

Trees are often, to little boys, what the beanstalk was to Jack. The urge to climb up a branch or two, then the next time, higher and higher. There was the thrill of achieving a climb, to be able to look down through the leaves at your friends below. Now it was your space, to share only with the birds and squirrels.

When your mother came out to call you, to remind you not to leave the yard, and then she could not find you even though you were there all the time, looking down on her standing, holding the broom and dustpan.

Some Eau Claire boys were lucky enough to have a tree house or a platform resting between two large branches. Social clubs were held in the tree houses with rules and passwords before you could enter. Often smaller brothers or girls were not admitted to these secret organizations.

In the small channel beside Prince's Island, someone in the distant past had hung a rope from a branch of a large poplar tree. Many boys had swung out over the water on that rope, arching out over the water then to jump off close to the bank, so that your feet would not get trapped in the mud on the bottom.

There were other large trees on the island that we nailed pieces of wood on to form a ladder in order to gain access to the sitting branches. Here, two or three boys could balance and discuss the affairs of life.

Near the rapids on the south side of the river, was a grove of young poplar trees. They were such that if you climbed the branches carefully, you could get close to the top, and because the trees were green and flexible, you could hang on as your weight bent the stem over to return you to the ground. If you wonder why all those trees had a bend in them, there is your answer.

There was a large poplar in the yard next to 711. As you looked out the bedroom window in the early morning, the sun's rays shone through the tree's branches. Each morning in May you could see the buds open up into leaves and the tree get greener and greener; Oh the magic of spring.

Climbing up Telephone Poles

There were some telephone or power poles in the Eau Claire that had metal steps along each side that were used to get up to the wires. For little boys there was always the dare to climb to the top. However, that was a long way up, or to put it another way, it was a long way down the higher up you got.

Buddy would climb up four steps, I would go up five. Buddy would then climb up six steps, I would go up five. Buddy would then climb up six steps and I wanted to go one above that. Again a climb, one foot above the other, hanging on the higher steps with both hands, four steps, then five; don't look down, then carefully on to the sixth step. The wind seemed to be whistling in my ears, the pole seemed to be moving; hang tight, don't fall, better get down; at least you tied Buddy.

Just then, Tommy came down the street. "I can go higher than that," he yelled. Up he went, five, six, seven, eight, nine, ten, almost to the top. Although we wanted to, we did not try to beat his record.

Closets

There was only one real closet at 711 Eau Claire Avenue. It was in the front upstairs bedroom, and we did not often get to use if because that room, and sometimes the whole upstairs was rented out in order for my parents to meet the monthly rent.

What did we use for clothing storage space? Well, Dad put up rods across the corners in two rooms, hung curtains from them, and clothes were hung on hooks or nails along the wall.

There were hooks near the back door to hold kid's jackets. Boots, gloves, mitts hats and scarves were piled on the floor beneath.

In the hallway beside the front door were two hooks for Mom's fur collared winter coat as well as Dad's heavy and threadbare tweed coat.

There was always the smell of mothballs anywhere woolen clothing was stored.

Clotheslines

Every house in Eau Claire had one or more clotheslines, normally stretching from the house to the back of the yard. Some lines would be reached from the back porch, some had their own step-up-to, and the odd one was adjacent to an open window. Most of the lines were operated on a pulley system where the clothes could be pulled in or out from the landing.

Some householders were not as fortunate as the line, be it wire or cord, was just strung from one nail or post to another.

Clothespins were stored in a tin can nailed to the post or there were clothes bags, often embroidered by the owner.

Monday was normally designated as 'wash day'. By noon the lines were hung with clothes and sheets, hopefully flapping and drying in the wind, but not in a dust storm.

As a matter of pride those sets of long underwear or other apparel were hung so that the gossiping or critical neighbours would not see the holes or tears. Winter time saw the clothes and sheets freeze solid, which proved to be extra work and frozen fingers as the stiff washing was removed from the line.

Clotheslines were also used to air blankets and rugs. Sons and daughters were sent out with the kitchen broom or a wire rug beater to beat the dust and dirt out of the rugs.

The Coal Delivery

"Billy, get right home after school; the coal is being delivered today."

I knew that this would be a lot of hard work, but Mom would reward me.

Last time, the coal had been delivered by a horse drawn wagon. This time an old truck with solid rubber tires was dumping a large load of coal beside the house. Most houses on the block had gas furnaces, but 711 still burned coal, although our kitchen stove and the living room heater used natural gas.

Part of our basement was a coal room, and its small window had been removed so that I could throw the coal down.

I got my old wagon and began piling the smaller pieces on, hoping my father or my sisters would help with the larger pieces that I could hardly lift.

I pulled the wagon close to the window and unloaded chunk after chunk of coal, heaving the lumps into the basement window and trying not to hit the wooden frame.

Did I get tired - yes; did I get dirty - yes; did I get coal dust under my fingernails and in my eyes - yes!

Finally, my Mom came out with a bread, butter and sugar sandwich and a glass of home made lemonade.

"Enjoy these Billy; you have worked hard. Your father will finish the rest."

By the next year, a gas fitter had come and changed the coal furnace into a gas furnace.

Coal Oil

"Billy, take this nickle and run up to the service station and get me a bottle of coal oil. Now be careful; don't drop the bottle or fall down and cut your hands."

The bottle was an empty whiskey bottle, the size of which my father called a double mickey. The bottle had probably been picked up along the river.

Out the back door, through the alley and up Sixth Street I ran. The Snow Cap Service Station was four blocks away, on the North West corner of fourth Avenue and Sixth Street.

The coal oil was pumped out of a barrel, and they would let me fill the bottle myself. Afterwards, if it were needed, I would pump up to fill the twenty-gallon gasoline containers at the top of the pumps. The glass containers were marked to show how much gasoline would be put in a car. Not an absolute accurate measurement, but that is the way it was done.

Back home, down Sixth Street, but with side trip and distractions along the way.

"Billy, where have you been? I sent you for the coal oil a half an hour ago."

Coal oil was used as a cleaning fluid. Because we pronounced it as 'coiloil', it was years later that I finally realized what it was.

A Cold bottle of Pop

One of the great joys for Eau Claire kids on a hot summer day was a cold bottle of pop. Even better were two bottles. The store cost was five cents a bottle, while large bottles of Canada Dry Ginger Ale sold for 25 cents. All regular bottles were 12 ounces, except Seven-up and Orange Crush that were ten ounces.

Besides Coca Cola, which was not generally called coke, other pops were: the Calgary Brewing's Big Orange, Big Lemon and Big Lime, Seven-up, Lime Rickey, Pepsi Cola, Blue Label's Stubby, and the bottles were stubby, of many flavours including grape and cream soda. There was a time when ginger beer, in stone bottles, could be found.

For a beer or a pop bottle the Blue Label bottling plant, located on Third Avenue, would allow you to drink a bottle of unsaleable pop. This could be a bottle not quite filled, or too weak or too strong. Bring two empties in and you could take it with you or else you drank it there right in the back room beside the bottling machinery.

Once or twice a year the Coca Cola Company, located on Fourth Avenue near Chinatown, would sponsor special days where, if you brought a ticket found in the newspaper, they would give you a Coca Cola and a bright red hat with the words 'Coca Cola' printed in white letters on each side.

Some Eau Claire boys would go house to house asking for the tickets from the Herald and then literally bloat themselves on too much pop.

The Cold Box

Keeping food cool in the hot days of summer was a problem in the Eau Claire, as it was for most families. Some households had an icebox and ice could be delivered weekly. 711 had a circular box with a lid that was buried in the shady area of the front yard. This was not the only underground food container found in the Eau Claire or Calgary for that matter.

Mom did not use it a great deal, but if there were vegetables, fruits or food that she was concerned about she would put the food in a pail, put a cover on it and lower it into the box. Being about three feet below ground did well in keeping the food cool.

The box was also used by little boys as a dare - who would accept a dare and lower one's self into the cool clammy pit knowing the lid could be closed, the clasp fitted, and you were trapped. Yes, it did happen, but boys will be boys.

Coloured Folk

Since I was very young, I had played with Indian children, out either on the reserve or when they visited 711. There were children of many nationalities in the Eau Claire, including Jewish boys and girls who seemed to have a different way of life.

One day I met Dennis. Dennis was black. Some might say coloured, but the work coloured did not seem to exist in the Eau Claire. Not only was the colour of his skin unique but also as much was his laughter and a smile 'a mile wide.' You could not be with Dennis for more than a few seconds, you were giggling, and laughing at that heaven only knows.

Dennis's mother was in control of her son and he knew the boundary of behaviour and the exploration of the Eau Claire. However, Dennis enjoyed baseball, and his skills in this sport were better than mine. His mother knew he was not getting into trouble when he played baseball with me.

Company Houses

North of Eau Claire Avenue and for a short block west of Fourth Street was a small road known as Centre Avenue. On the north side of this dirt road was a group of company houses belonging to the Eau Claire Lumber Company. The houses were small, perhaps 20 feet by 30, all of the same design and they backed on the mud hole stream. The houses were occupied by the employees of the sawmill, which was just east of fourth Street.

Cowboys and Indians

The trees along the river took a beating as we stripped branches to make bows and arrows for one of our games of 'Cowboys and Indians'. The stress placed on the weak poplar branch meant that a bow's life was very short.

Who were the good guys and who were the bad, it did not generally matter, and most kids easily changed from one role to another on a daily basis.

One of the good points of this activity was the allowable noise level, be it cap guns, "giddap, get them up, bang, you're dead", or shrieks or war hoops from the Indians.

Sometimes the real fight cries started when someone was captured and hands tied too tight, and then there was anger, arguing, crying and taunts.

Mothers made Indian costumes out of gunny sacking. Backyard chicken coops provided plenty of feathers. Mother's or big sister's make-up provided lots of face decoration colour.

Cowboy outfits included straw hats, neck bandanas, gun holsters and, what is not often seen today, wrist gauntlets.

Smaller children rode their broomstick horses. The McLennan's were one up because we had our own Shetland pony, but its use was not allowed in the Cowboy and Indian battles.

The Creaking Door

Calgary's three radio stations provided some good drama during the winter evenings. Probably the scariest of these was "The Creaking Door". It started and ended with that very scary and mysterious noise of a creaking door. Often this sound was used in the story to create suspense and fear. These stories brought shivers and fright to a small boy. The story seemed to spill out of the radio and be part of our house. You were very careful about listening to these gruesome tales if you were home alone.

There were times after the show when my mother would ask me to go down into the cellar to get some potatoes or to dig some carrots from the sand in which they were stored in for the winter. The feelings from "The Creaking Door" remained with me as I walked to the dark, back corner where the vegetables were stored. Then with the pan filled, I literally ran back up the stairs before a claw reached out to grab me.

Creativity

Creativity came in simple ways for the children of Eau Claire to express themselves. One such way was rock decorating and painting. The Bow River contained an endless supply of rocks of all shapes, sizes and colours. Basically, we used crayons to create designs, but if we were able to stockpile several colours of house paint gathered at garbage cans then we were able to do designs on larger rocks that had some permanence. The rocks, upon completion and drying, would be thrown into the river, to what we hoped would be of interest and colour for visitors to the Bow.

Vegetation was also used for creativity and self- expression. Besides those quick and temporary dandelion rings, we made strings of beads once the rose hips were ripe enough to pick. This meant borrowing a needle and thread from Mom, picking the rose hips and carefully threading, perhaps a hundred long into a necklace.

The results; well a sense of accomplishment, temporary wearing, perhaps a gift to Mom, but mostly a project accomplished.

Sometimes, at the risk of cut fingers, we would borrow the butcher knife and cut designs in the soft wood branches of the river poplars. We sometimes tried to make whistles this way, but not with any success.

Periodically we would hike to the steep hillside east of Centre Street Bridge. Here were open clay banks and we would collect clay, carefully picking for texture, and carrying it home in a jam tin or bag.

We spent considerable time working out a suitable texture and density to shape it into pots and other crude shapes. We were only moderately successful, but there was satisfaction in trying.

Crystal Skating Rink and Swimming Pool

The Crystal Skating Rink, built and owned by Andy Baxter, a former professional baseball player, had at one time been located on Seventh Avenue. However, during my childhood it was located on Fourth Avenue, east of Louise Bridge and west of the Premier Laundry. There was a high fence around the main and the back rink, but there were windows, covered with chicken wire, along the Fourth Avenue fence. When there was skating taking place there were almost always spectators looking through the windows.

The skate or changing room area was located over the swimming pool, which for the winter season was covered with supports and planking. A small room, which overlooked the main rink, housed the record player and public address system, from which would emit the delightful strains of the skater's waltz or other music of the era. The 78 speed records became scratchier as the season wore on.

Nightly, from seven until ten, there was public skating. Besides free skate there were times 'only for pairs , sometimes there was 'lady's' or 'men's' choices. If it were 'lady's the boys would hide, or vice versa the girls. However, secretly, we all hoped that someone would ask us to skate.

Sometimes the rink would allow 'crack the whip' where hand in hand a long line of skaters would be pulled by a pivot skater so that the line of skaters would be spun around the ice with the outer skaters moving at an accelerated speed to sometimes fly off the end of the chain or go down on the ice to slide into the boards.

The back rink was smaller and was generally used for fancy (figure) skating or for practise by the speed skaters. From this rink Ralph Olin, the first Calgarian to compete in speed skating in the Winter Olympics, emerged.

After the skating ended a long, black hose would be brought out on to the ice to flood it. Because of its size, there was a lot of snow shoveling to be done after a snowstorm: local boys received skate entrance credit for offering a helping hand.

The cost of an evening or afternoon's skating at the Crystal was 10 cents for children and 25 cents for adults, Small amounts, but not always possible to come up with for many Calgarians of the era.

The Crystal Swimming Pool

After the outdoor ice had melted, Mr. Baxter and his crew removed the flooring and supports from the swimming pool. The cement pool was perhaps forty feet wide by a hundred feet long - a shallow end and a deep end. Here were three diving boards, low, medium and high. The pool also had a blown up tractor tire and a rope to swing out on.

The water was not exactly warm and it was very heavily chlorinated. The dressing rooms were smelly and dreary. However, the pool was here, thanks to Andy Baxter.

Sometimes he would walk into the pool area, and, taking a hand full of pennies from his pocket, he would throw them into the pool for the deep divers to retrieve.

Curiosity Corner - The Odd Shaped House

On the south side of First Avenue, between Seventh and Eight Street was a house in which the west side came to an acute point. It was at this location that First Avenue curved south to join into Second Avenue. After construction had started on the house, the city informed the owner of the planned realignment of First Avenue.

The house became to be known as Curiosity Corner.

Cutting Grass

Mechanical lawn mowers might be seen in the Mechanic's Illustrated magazine, but certainly not in the Eau Claire. Even Buffalo Stadium, with its large grassy outfield, had to be cut by hand.

Those of Eau Claire who did have grass and a hand pushed lawn mower, could be seen and heard sharpening the blades with a stone before the lawn was cut. Small boys could be recruited to push a mower, but this often meant a running start into the long grass and, with luck, five feet of cutting.

The Dairy

The Producer's Milk Dairy, located on Third Avenue and Fifth Street, had their butter plant and the stables in another two story building on First Avenue, just off of Sixth Street. The yard, which was entered on Second Avenue, also was used for wagon storage. During the day, when the wagons were in service, the yard was a good playground for the neighbourhood children. We often played (baseball) grounders on the smooth dirt. However a bad throw might put the baseball into the manure pile in the corner.

The horses were put two in a stall. After walking the streets of Calgary since the early morning there were content to munch their hay, which was dropped into the bins from the hay storage area on the second floor. Sometimes we were allowed to brush and curry some of the quieter horses.

In the summer we would help lead the horses to the river for a drink and a wade. However if we let a horse roll in the mud the verbal sparks would fly.

In a room fronting on First Avenue the butter, which came over from the dairy in tubs, was cut into pound blocks and wrapped in wax paper by hand. Sometimes flies got in from the barn, but a fly swatter was kept handy.

Decorated Houses at Christmas

When you walked in Eau Claire at Christmas, you might see the lights on a Christmas tree shining through a window. Sometimes a large paper wreath would be hung on the front door. Outside, decorations were few and far between, but on occasion, a wooden outline of Santa might appear on a roof.

One December evening, my father said that we were going to see the Christmas lights that were hung outside on people's houses. Try as I might, I could not imagine how coloured lights could be placed outside.

Anyway, all six of us dressed extra warm and piled into the car, and then blankets were wrapped around our legs. Dad drove over the Louise Bridge and up the hill where we often went for a sleigh ride. There was a line of cars ahead of us driving slowly in order to see the lights.

As we inched along Crescent Road, the lights came into view. Strings of coloured lights had been placed along the eaves of at least six houses. There must have been hundreds of lights: red, green, yellow, blue and white, all alight. Father drove down to the end of the block, past many walkers who had come out to see this display. He turned around and we got back in the slow parade to see the lights from the other side of the car.

The next year there were many houses in the city that had outside Christmas lights, but those on Crescent Road were Calgary's first.

Depression Furniture

Wooden boxes played an important role in the furnishings of many Eau Claire houses. Sunkist orange crates had a divider to use as a shelf. Some curtain, a bit of paint, and you had a bedside table, a bookcase or to be used as storage for food.

Apple boxes were solid and could be used the same way.

However, additional uses saw them used as dirty clothes boxes, vegetable storage or a toy box. Butter boxes were strong, solid and being a cube, might be used as a footstool or a table in front of the sofa.

More than one Eau Claire child slept on a small wooden bed made by the father. Winnipeg couches were used as sofas during the day, but turned into a bed at night.

Washing machines, if a family had one, were often in the kitchen. Ours served as a breadbox, except on Monday when washing took place.

How often a picture from the cover of the Star Weekly, Ladies Home Journal or other magazines found its way to be tacked on the wall for additional decoration.

Wooden high chairs might have been used by several children, and had probably been passed down from another generation.

Perhaps many of the projects that were turned out at the McDougall School manual training classes might be considered depression projects, for often was used lumber utilized, and the skills were basic. These projects were ideal as Christmas or birthday presents, and parents would proudly display them in the home.

Depression Lawn Ornaments

Many home gardens and flowerbeds in the Eau Claire area were inset with tin cans; the top and bottom cut out and generally, the labels were removed. These cans were used to provide shelter and protection for some types of flowers and vegetables. It made watering easier, provided a little protection from a late frost and allowed the sun's heat to collect.

Tomato cans were favoured, for they were as wide as they were deep. Some gardeners thought that the metal of the cans enriched the soil. The cans would also protect the small plants from birds and animals.

Old tires were often used in flowerbeds to give shape and form around patches of flowers. The width of the tire rim was smaller and the cases were weaker in strength, so the tires could be half sunk into the ground. Many people gave the tires a coat of white paint.

Vegetable gardens, which most yards had at least a patch of, often contained a scarecrow. Old pants, and they had to very old in the Eau Claire, a raggedy shirt, gloves on the end of stick arms and an old hat on the top of the upright piece of the cross frame helped to complete the scarecrow.

There were birdhouses and whirligigs, bird wings revolving, men sawing wood and women washing clothes in a tub.

On the corner of Second Avenue and Fourth Street was, in the eyes of an Eau Claire child, a lovely cottage, surrounded by a wire fence and enclosed in a yard of beautiful trees and bushes. This was all fine, but to add additional pleasure for the passer-by were birdhouses of every size, design and colour. On top of the clotheslines and other poles were whirligigs, dipping and swirling whenever there was a breeze.

This lovely yard was just across the street from the Thorpe House, which sits in Heritage Park. This brings me fond memories of both houses.

Dog Bones

"Billy, the dog is hungry and we are out of scraps. You had better go and get some dog bones."

"Yes Mom, I am on the way." Always happy to run someplace I took off for the Safeway store on Fourth Street, just south of Fifth Avenue.

The meat counter ran along the south side of the store, and at the back end was a huge cold storage room. Beside its door was the box full of bones and scraps from the days cutting. I found a cardboard box and filled it with as many bones and scraps that I could carry. On the way home, if it were a warm day, the box and I attracted many flies.

Finally, I arrived home, arms weary, and I was anxious for a drink of cold water. The dog smelled the bones and came running. Sometimes Mom found a good soup bone in the box and added it to her stew, often made of vegetables from her garden.

Billy, Bobby and Sport,

Frank McCool, the Toronto Maple Leaf goalie, grew up in the large house across the street.

Dressing Sport Up

One cold and snowy winter day, we got the bright idea to put some clothes on Sport, our crossbreed, but mainly German Shepherd dog.

We found an old sweater, with moth holes and worn holes on the elbows. Mom said that we could use it, but she did not really approve of our project, nor did she believe that it would work.

Anyway, Bobby held Sport and I worked at fitting the sweater over his head, which was the easy part, and then one arm over one leg and then really stretching the sweater to cover the other leg. Thank goodness the sweater stretched. The sleeves were too long so we rolled them up. Now we were ready to brave the elements and display our well-dressed dog to the Eau Claire.

Now, Sport had a few enemies amongst the canine population of the Eau Claire. We walked to Parkin's corner, and all of a sudden, there were two large and unfriendly dogs at our backside, snarling with teeth bared. Sport turned, and with his back fur raised, took after them, but by now, the sleeves were down covering his paws.

With the sweater being easy to sink their teeth in to, the dogs pulled and shook the sweater, which was pulled over Sport's head. We found a stick and beat the dogs off. Sport tried to take off after them, but he could not see and the sleeves hobbled him.

We managed to take the sweater, or what was left of it, off him and home we went.

My mother's words were, "You never learn, do you?"

Easter Entertainment at the Legion

As most schoolchildren do, the arrival of Easter was looked forward to, as there were Easter eggs, a week off of school and fun filled afternoons at the Legion on Seventh Avenue East.

Here was a week of entertainment for free, no strings attached. It seemed like every kid in Calgary was there and the place was packed.

After everyone quieted down, we listened to Maude Riley, and elderly lady dressed in black and wearing a hat, talk to us on our responsibilities of life, about being good to others, obeying the law, working hard at school and helping out at home.

This would be followed by the entertainment. There were tap dancers, jugglers, singing groups and tumblers. All good in themselves, but the best was yet to come.

A movie projector was set up in the middle of the floor, the screen pulled down and the lights turned off. The movies, in black and white of course, were most often Castle Films, cartoons, cartoons and cartoons. Felix the Cat was often the main character and the plots were often very similar. Charlie Chaplin, Laurel and Hardy and Tom Mix were other actors that filled the screen.

It was great fun for the week instead of school. We were out of our mother's hair and she knew we were in good hands. Besides the entertainment, there was the adventure of the trip downtown and then home again.

Eau Claire Architecture

The architecture of the Eau Claire could only be described as eclectic. Its jewel would be McDougall School, opened in 1906 as the Normal School. Its shape and size in the eyes of a child appeared very regal. The impressive front steps, columns and large windows contributed to an air of distinction.

A step down on the architectural hierarchy was the Connaught, a red brick apartment with two main entrances and balconies, which was located on Fourth Avenue north of the school. The Saddam Court, a lovely six apartment complex, with a stone fence was located on Fifth Avenue, and one block south was the El Palo, the closest that Calgary's architecture came to the mystique of Latin architecture.

Of lesser beauty was the Commercial Dairy, on Third Avenue and Fifth Street. The structure was U shaped and there was a courtyard to store the dairy wagons.

The Alberta Laundry and Alberta Printing were two, two story buildings that stretched from First Avenue to Second Avenue. Both buildings had many windows, too often broken. The Ontario, another red brick laundry was located on Fourth Avenue and Eighth Street.

Eau Claire contained some magnificent brick houses, mainly on Fourth Avenue. Perhaps the 'prince' of them was the Prince House. Further west was the residence of Turner-Bone, On the south side of Fourth was the Braemar Lodge, a long two-story brick building with some beautiful leaded glass windows.

There were large three story houses on Second, Third and Fourth Avenues. Many had been converted into apartments or rooming houses. These structures had multiple entrances, long hallways and small rooms; bathrooms were mostly shared. Bath times were often designated, and clothes washing was often in a tub.

There were many two-story houses, the front door on the left or right side opening into the staircase to the second floor. Some of these houses contained two suites, one up and the other down. Basements were often just cellars.

Most of the Eau Claire homes, built between 1900 and 1914, had a front veranda, wicker chairs and a Virginia creeper vine. Some of the houses had a barrel shaped cold storage container that was sunk in the ground.

Some of the houses were bungalows, but under the roof would be a small room with one or two dormer windows. Children would have access to these small bedrooms by a staircase that was more like a ladder.

Interspersed throughout the neighbourhood were some structures that were more like shacks; no basements, lean-tos, stovepipe chimneys, doors that led directly into rooms, and in some cases only one door.

With few exceptions, every house had a clothesline, sometimes two, and the rooming houses double that. Garages were smaller, often converted barns. The double doors were wooden hinged on the side and locked with a bar attached to the inside of one door and was swung to fit in a notch on the other door.

Chicken coops, yes, often attached to the garage. There were many pigeon coops, some on the garage roofs, some made of chicken wire behind the garage and the odd one on stilts.

The Eau Claire architecture truly contained a diversification of architecture that under future city zoning and building by-laws would not have happened.

Eau Claire as the Apex

To us 'riverbank kids', the Eau Claire district was the centre of the world. We could see the rim of the north hill, hear the whistle of the Ontario Laundry in East Calgary and the Armouries and Mewata Park to the west.

True, we walked the railway line to Brickburn, rode the streetcar to Bowness Park, the Zoo and to the Arena at the Exhibition Grounds, but these were adventures into alien territory.

For myself the trip to the library in Central Park, by way of the railroad crossing on fourth Street, past the statue of the eagle perched on the top of the building on Tenth Avenue, beside the war statues in the park and to the library, was in itself an adventure for a small child.

As one grew older, the boundaries of my world grew wider and I learned a new perspective. Every day can produce, perhaps a small, but a new adventure.

Eau Claire Churches

Churches and religion were, in many respects, part of the social and cultural life of the boys and girls of Eau Claire.

For some of us, there was the magnificent gothic like edifice of Knox United Church, which meant Sunday school and Friday night Boys Club, with lots of indoor games and sports. The girls had C.G.I.T., Canadian Girls in Training. The Christmas concerts and the summer picnics at Bowness Park were two very important social events for children. The Knox boys could also participate in a Canada wide multi event of athletic skills of which the local competition was held at Mewata Stadium.

There were other churches in the area that we visited. On Third Avenue and Eighth Street was the Trinity Lutheran Church, which had its beginning at this location in 1899 as the Scandinavian Lutheran Church. Here at Christmas we would peer in the windows to see a wondrous candlelight procession. Other times, out of curiosity, we might visit Mount Calvary Lutheran, located on Third Street and Fourth Avenue.

Periodically, we walked to Centre Street and the Christadelphia Church and the mystery of it, or to the House of Jacob on Fifth Avenue East.

Several blocks south of Eau Claire, on Seventh Avenue, was the Second Church of Christ Reading Room, where we could read newspapers printed in far away locations.

There was the Scandinavian Mission Church located in a very plain building at 510 Fifth Street, but other than the Sunday Service, it seemed to remain closed and dark.

Part of the time, I and some of my buddies, visited a small apartment above Lintick's Meat Market, located on Third Avenue. Here we sat on the sofa and listened to Bible readings, knowing that there would be cake or cookies afterwards

We cannot forget the walks uptown to listen to the street corner band concerts and sermons of the Salvation Army.

The Eau Claire Country Club

It may not, in reality, have been a country club, but for boys, such as me, it was a recreation from heaven that allowed for sports and play, an easy way to earn pocket money, entertainment and a great place to hang out.

A sincere thank you to J. B. Cross and the Calgary Brewing and Malting Company for the baseball park known as Buffalo Stadium that was created and built on land north of First Avenue between Fifth and Sixth Streets. Prior to that time the land had been a parade square for the naval training station, H.M.C.S. Tecumseh, and long before that was the site of a log storage pond for the saw mill.

The Buffalo complex served as the home of Calgary's senior baseball league in the summer, while in the winter three hockey rinks were used by the Buffalo Athletic Association Hockey League, and as well, were offered for public skating to music each evening until 10 P.M.

When the park opened in the early 1940's it proved to be an absolute delight to the baseball crowd, as the previously used field, located on the west side of Mewata Stadium was in a sad state of repair.

Buffalo Stadium's home plate was situated in the northeast corner of the park, and a foul ball hit from here could end up in the bushy area around the mud hole, or the water itself. The outfield fence did not follow the usual arch of a baseball field, but instead it worked its way around a building, which had been a puffed wheat factory but now was the Alberta Casket Company. The eight-foot fence was covered with panels of advertisements for various Calgary businesses. Something that was unique in Calgary's sports facilities.

Weekend games would often see complete sell-outs of the bleacher's seats, and after they were full, the fans and spectators were allowed to sit on the grass, sometimes three deep, along the outfield fence. This was considered a natural hazard of play. Any ball that ended up unplayable in that area was considered a two base hit.

Some of the local kids, including myself, were batboys for the various teams. Besides a nifty uniform to wear there were cracked bats and old balls to take home, as well as a pop at the end of the game. Best of all I had a chance to pitch batting practise or shag balls in the outfield.

Within the ballpark, there were several jobs in the concessions. Best job of all on a hot day was selling pop, manufactured by the Calgary Brewery of course. Big Orange, Big Lemon, and Big Lime were available at ten cents each, two cents to the seller, and often sold as fast as you could uncap them. Hot dog and cushion sales were not as lucrative.

Admission to the games was 25 cents, except for Sunday games, which, because of an enforced Lord's Day Act, were silver collection.

Besides two local clubs, there were teams from the local armed forces bases, including an American team. Teams from U.S. military bases in Montana, Alaska, whose rosters included major league players, flew in to Calgary for exhibition games. One late season game that was played before a capacity crowd featured the local all-stars against a touring team of 'National League All-Stars'

The kids that hung around the park were aware that Dutch, who was a handyman around the park, had been a great player in the National Hockey League, but was now in a position where he now used a broom or a shovel, and this transformation was difficult to understand.

Another individual that drew kids notice was the umpire, Henry Viney, who seemed as wide as he was tall, yet he seemed to run to first base as fast as the players. Henry went on to become one of the city's premier sports announcers.

In the winter, the local kids again used the park as a hangout. Although there were many hockey games scheduled there, it seemed that there was always one sheet of ice left for shinny. Stomach and arm muscles were hardened with all the scraping and shoveling to keep the three rinks clear of snow. Flooding was done by hose. Adding a new topping of water was an arduous job as a water barrel, mounted on wheels and pushed by a handle wide enough for two pair of hands; spread a thin coat of water through gunnysacks behind the barrel.

In the evenings, one rink was generally used for pleasure skating. A public address system, with large speakers attached to the fence played records and included music by Glen Miller and Tommy Dorsey.

Parents generally knew that their children were over at the stadium, but it was not unusual to see and hear an irate parent whose child had stayed out beyond the bedtime hour.

A hangout, yes, mischief, pushing and shoving, at times, a sense of belonging and a home away from home, yes.

Buffalo Stadium was indeed our 'country club'

The Eau Claire International Club

There were some evenings and weekend days when the accents of New Zealand, Australia, Britain and various Canadian Maritimers could be heard in the backyard of 711 Eau Claire Avenue. My father was in the Air Force and stationed at the Currie Flying School. He owned a car, was able to get some gasoline in this time of ration so it was much easier to bring home some of the outsiders who were in training here.

The airmen would often arrive with some food and some bottles of beer, and the evening's socialization would be full of chatter and laughter. As well, for me, there were more beer bottles to sell at Blue Label.

Some of the men, some still teenagers, would be happy to play catch with me or play soccer with a tennis ball. My sisters owned bicycles and some of the airmen enjoyed a ride around the block.

After their training the airmen went overseas to fly Lancaster's, Spitfires and Hurricanes over Europe. Years later, my parents visited some of the airmen at their homes in the Maritimes.

Eau Claire Sawmill

The story of the Eau Claire mill has been written many times, and so this is an attempt to describe those aspects of the mill that relate to the river and the Eau Claire district.

After the company obtained the timber rights on 100 square miles of land adjacent to the Bow, Kananaskis and Spray rivers, land for the location of the mill was obtained. Two logging camps were established, one on the Bow at Silver City and the other on the Kananaskis. In Calgary, a log weir was placed adjacent to the mill site.

Upstream from the island, a log channel was created. In addition, a log weir constructed on its north side and further upstream another weir was placed across the main stream of the Bow.

Machinery for the mill was brought to Calgary and set up in 1886. By this time, log drives were taking place on the Bow River, with gangs of up to forty men moving the logs from the mountains to Calgary. Peavey poles were used to move the key logs and open up the logjams.

Logs were from eight to sixteen inches in diameter and were cut in 12, 14 and 16-foot lengths.

Log drives took place on the Bow from 1886 to 1944. The mill ceased operation the following year. In its top producing year the mill turned out three carloads of lumber daily, and it was the main source of lumber in the Calgary area.

Gradually, improvements were made to the log run; timber shored up the south bank near the west bridge; a bridge was constructed to connect the mill to the island and west of the island another bridge and a water screen connected the gravel bar to the island. Another small bridge crossed the Bow just west of Sixth Street.

An office was constructed in the mill yard. The lumber was stacked to cure and filled the huge yard.

In 1889, the Calgary Water Power Company's plant was opened adjacent to the mill. A new weir was placed across the Bow west of Tenth Street. This helped to raise and regulate the water level to produce a drop of 13 feet. 700 horsepower and 60 kilowatts were obtained during peak operations. In the winter a steam plant, fuelled by coal and waste from the sawmill, replaced the water source. The Calgary Water Power Company was purchased by the Calgary Power Company.

Many of the employees of the sawmill made their home in the Eau Claire District. The mill owners constructed the six houses on Centre A Avenue.

Many Calgarians would visit the Bow to see the arrival of the log run in the spring. The logs were dangerous to play on, but running on them, spinning a log until you fell off and riding a log down the river were great sources of fun and excitement for many a Eau Claire boy.

Eau Claire sawmill and the power plant

Eau Claire office

The sawmill and wood scrap piles

An Eau Claire Sunday

Was Sunday in the Eau Claire that much different from the other days of the week? Yes, very much so.

It was much quieter; no whistles from the sawmill or the laundries, no screech of the sawmill saw, no clip-clop of the delivery wagons and fewer streetcars on Fourth Avenue.

Morning was generally of a sober nature as families slept in, then prepared for church. From afar came the faint ringing of church bells.

Clotheslines were, for the most part empty, because it was the Lord's Day, and it wan not for housework, except cooking.

Prior to driving to church, and cars were certainly not a part of every household, fathers could, while dressed in suit pants and a white shirt, take a bucket of water and wipe off the car windows.

Mothers wore a hat and perhaps a fox stole to church, but for the most part the Eau Claire people were not well off and many of the children wore hand-me-downs or send hand clothing.

After church there might be a walk to the river, or if there was a ball game at Buffalo Stadium, a visit there, because Sunday was silver collection.

Many children went skating or to play hockey at the Buffalo, Crystal or McDougall rinks. Many families did not encourage their children to participate in Sunday sports or play.

Wives often met at the back fence to gossip with their neighbours. It was Sunday; let peace and good will prevail.

From a commercial point of view, the 'Lord's Day Act' was in force and was strictly enforced. The grocery stores were closed and confectionaries were only allowed to sell certain goods, which were listed on a posted sign. There were no Sunday movies and admission to sports events was by silver collection.

Often on a Sunday, I would travel with my parents, my father driving his dilapidated Essex, up the Seventeenth Avenue hill, across the prairie, over the old wooden bridge at Weasel Head and up to our friends on the Sarcee Reserve.

I played with the Indian children, rode their horses, tried to ride the calves and socialized in the way of most small children.

Expanding Our Horizons

As a child grows and hopefully matures, the worldly boundaries expand to include further glimpses of life beyond Eau Claire.

Sunnyside could be seen across the river; Hillhurst was entered when your parents took you to Riley Park. However these areas were really yours when you could cross Louise Bridge, and with coins in your pocket, enter the Dairy Rich, climb up on one of the metal stools to read all of the milk shake flavours, the variety of sodas, sundaes and banana splits. What a choice!

The hard decision was whether to buy a milkshake for 10 cents, or splurge and have a 15-cent sundae or a large magnificent banana split for 25 cents.

There were many other stores on Tenth Street. There was Piggly Wiggly, which later became Safeway, shoe stores, clothing stores, a hardware, a bank and a drug store. On the west side was a feed store that used to buy minnows from us to sell to fishermen for bait.

Above the stores in the two story brick buildings lived older people, often seen looking out their windows onto the street with streetcars and delivery wagons passing by.

As we got older, Mom would send us down to McGavin's Bakery on Tenth Street, where we could smell the new baked goods and buy a loaf of day old bread for a nickel.

The Factory

On the northeast corner of First Avenue and Sixth Street was located a one story building surrounded by a wire fence with the yard lined by poplar trees. The building occupied part of the block that was otherwise the location of Buffalo Stadium, whose outfield fence took a peculiar jag around the factory.

The building was occupied by a casket maker and the sight of coffins brought about thoughts of ghosts, and if you had to pass it in the evening, it was generally at a run, with a glance over your shoulder to see that there was not a sheet-shrouded figure behind you.

Later the building was the home to a puffed wheat factory. For 25 cents you could have a flour sack or a pillowcase filled with puffed wheat. As I walked home with this featherweight bag of cereal, my hand would delve in time and time again to fill my mouth with this magically created cereal. It was difficult to understand how a small hard grain of wheat could be transformed into a large light delicacy.

The puffed wheat factory was also a favourite roost of the local pigeons that would hover around the door to feast on fallen kernels.

Fences

Most of the yards in the Eau Claire area were fenced and most had a front gate. Many other yards had a caragana hedge, often full of chirping sparrows. The wire fences were very similar in construction, with strands of interwoven wire standing about shoulder height to a small boy.

The gates were often made of the same type of wire fastened to a tubular metal frame, with a latch on one side and metal decoration on the top.

Many yards had picket fences, generally whitewashed or painted white. If a homeowner had a long fence covering the front and the side street, they might use chicken wire. One large home in Eau Claire had a brick fence topped with tiles. We knew better than to venture into that yard to look for a lost ball. Do good fences make for better neighbours?

On Third Avenue there were fences built of rocks and cement. We called these the castle fences. One of our little games was to pick out the most beautiful rocks.

The back fence of one yard that backed onto the river was made of long pieces of lathing. Here is where we got the material to help in the construction of out river kayaks.

Buffalo Stadium's fences were eight feet high and surrounded the park. The centre field fence made several changes in direction to get around the puffed wheat factory. The fence was completely covered by many large commercial signs painted on the wood. They were bright, eye catching and good for reading between the innings.

Fire Alarms

Attached to the wooden street lampposts, at some street corners, were fire alarms. In order to activate and send a signal to the fire station a person had to just pull the handle down and the alarm was tripped. Because the fire might be two blocks from the alarm box, the person who set the alarm off would normally stay there to direct the firemen to the blaze. The fire truck could be heard by hand rung bells or a siren sounded by a hand turned handle.

One might ask, "Why a call would not be phoned in?" There were few phones in the Eau Claire district.

Sometimes, but not very often, a false alarm would be turned in, and the trucks would race to the alarm box, located either on First or Third Avenue. Later a policeman would show up in an attempt to determine the culprit.

One afternoon, a fire started in the remains of an old car that had been junked in the open land near the Bow River. Small boys who had built a bonfire on the front seat were responsible, but none of us could remember who started it.

One very cold afternoon, the sound of the fire truck's bells and a plume of dense smoke caused us to run towards the Armoury. On the south side of this castle like building, a large wooden hall was on fire; the structure consumed by flames. There was a huge crowd of spectators surrounding the blaze; the firemen had little success in saving the building.

One day my father said to me, "Come, Billy, lets go see the results of the prairie fire in Springbank."

He cranked the old Essex to start it and off we went, soon to be on the dusty gravel road heading west. Upon arrival at a farm, whose owner was a friend of my father, we were to find not a house, barn or shed left standing, no trees, bushes or stalks of brown fall grass. There were dead pigs, lying on their backs with their feet extended into the air. Numerous chickens, feathers singed off, littered the ground.

My father reminded me again, "Don't play with matches."

The First Fish I Really Caught

We caught lots of minnows in the mud ponds of the river; some were up to four inches long. Many suckers of a much larger size were caught at the weir or under the bridges, but I had never really caught a river fish on a line and a hook.

Yes, I had tried different types of hooks, various kinds of bait, different pools in the river, morning fishing, evening fishing, deep casts and casting, but to be honest, I had never caught a fish.

We could look into the murky water, gaze into the running water, see fish jumping from the pools, but never really catch one. There were many adults who fished from the shore or waded into the rapids and went home with one or two brown trout in their pouch, but not me.

One morning I decided to try my luck below the sawmill bridge. The bridge connected the mill property with Prince's Island. It stood high above the river, which at this point was deep and quiet.

On my hook, I placed a grasshopper. A nut from my father's workbench weighted down the gut. I had just dropped my line into the water when Deryk walked on to the bridge and asked, "How is the fishing?"

Just at that moment, a fish took the bait, and with a reflex action, I yanked up the rod, the force throwing the line and fish up into the air, over my back and onto the bridge. I scooped the fish up, banged its head on the boards, as if I had done it many times, to kill it.

"Fishing's good," I replied, carefully hiding the excitement of catching my first fish.

First Friend

Do you remember your first friend? For many children that was a Teddy Bear. For others it was a big brother or sister. To others it might have been the family dog or cat.

However, as one grew older there was always a special pride in telling Mom that you now had a friend! Perhaps you met them at the front gate or at the playground. Someone with whom you developed that kindred feeling, someone, other than your family, that you could communicate with, run and skip with, get down on your knees in the dirt with, or share your candy with. This was someone you just had to visit first thing in the morning, or that you stood and talked to as the evening rays of the sun diminished and Mom repeatedly called you to come in.

Yes, my first friend was a teddy bear, but with no attached arms or legs. I remember him sitting up front with me in the big truck that carried our furniture and goods from the house in Second Avenue to 711 Eau Claire. Now I was leaving my first true friend. Robin Scobert had lived across the street from me on Second Avenue, and whom I could see through the pickets of our fence. Our communication was first with our eyes, then shouts and simple words.

Later I got to know Robin, to visit his home, small and simple as it was, and to play with him. Soon he moved away, but he lives on as 'my first friend'.

First Skates

Sometime, about my age of seven, my father came home with a pair of old skates for me. They were a size or more too big, but cardboard liners, a lump of paper in the toe and two pair of darned socks made the fit a little more secure. The blades were one piece of forged steel, the kind that preceded tube skates.

What a thrill to have a pair of skates, to go to the rink and play some other position besides goal, a position reserved for those in shoes.

There was a city rink on the field located east of our house. The rink sided on First Avenue and Fifth Street.

The city put up the boards complete with angled corners. It did not have any lights and there was not a hockey shack.

Now, I will admit that it took me most of the season to learn to skate without being on my ankles.

Later the city flooded a rink on the McDougal School grounds. With an hour and a half for lunch there was always some time for hockey, a shinny game with twenty-a-side. If you were lucky or good, you touched the puck twice. Play would continue after school into the darkness or evening.

Feet grow and I was to own a pair of tube skates, not new and a tongue that had lost its sewing. It was every boy's goal to own a pair of Tacks, the top line of skates.

When the Calgary Brewing and Malting constructed Buffalo Stadium, between Fifth and Sixth Street, they flooded three rinks in the winter. There was almost always some ice for shinny or skating. There was a clean and warm room to tighten your skates in or buy a 'Big Orange', which was bottled by the brewery.

Florescent Paint

There was a magic shop on Eighth Avenue whose lure often called the boys of Eau Claire to visit it. There were so many magical goods in the store, but there was never enough money to buy them all. What about the spyglass that allowed you to look through walls, or the money finder that led you to coins in the grass. There were masks and kits that could turn you into a pirate. There were magic kits and books on how to play tricks on people.

One day I had enough money to buy a small bottle of florescent paint, guaranteed to shine in the dark. It was a very small bottle, so a great deal of thought was given to what should be painted with this magic paint.

Finally, I decided that I would paint the light bulb hanging on a cord from the ceiling in the bedroom I shared with my brother. I found a small paintbrush and stood on the bed to paint the bulb. At first, I could not see any difference, but after going to bed, and the darkness closed in, there was a noticeable glow to the bulb. As night came on, the brightness of the bulb increased, and it made sleep hard to come by.

Did my mother like it, no, was it a waste of a dime, yes.

Several days later, boys being boys, we had a pillow fight. Guess what, a pillow hit the light and we had glass all over. It took another week before Dad would replace the bulb.

A Fly or Flies

Flies were a nuisance at 711 and probably every other house in the Eau Claire district. Horse droppings and loose garbage contributed to fly breeding.

Most houses had screen doors to help keep flies out; never-the-less flies got in to buzz around and around the food and the light bulbs. In the basements and cellars, as well as garages, blue flies beat against the dirty glass windows seeking an escape.

Fly swatters were found in most households. Another popular weapon against these pests was flycatcher strips, long very sticky ribbons of paper, hung from the ceiling, and guaranteed to trap any fly that landed on its sticky surface. However, you were left with dead flies until the flycatcher was pulled down weeks, maybe months later.

Follow Your Dream

Eau Claire youngsters, as with most children, had dreams of their own, which they hoped to have fulfilled.

There were those who hoped to play professional hockey or baseball. There were those who hoped to go on to university and succeed in a profession. There were those who had job or career aspirations, and there were those whose dream was to get married and live happily thereafter.

What about the little dreams - to make a sports team, to own a bicycle, to graduate out of grade nine, to get a job and help your parents feed the family. There were dreams of finally having your own bedroom, not sharing it with one or two brothers. There were dreams of a new scooter or a pair of skates.

There were dreams of moving out of the Eau Claire, to a house with an electric fridge and an automobile in the driveway, to a trip on the train to Vancouver to see the ocean for real.

Many of these dreams were achieved by desire and hard work. As a Stanley Cup goalie learned his basic skills in the Eau Claire. A few boys went on to earn professional degrees at university. Many expanded their family business or developed their own business. Others excelled in the military or at the easel. Two of Eau Claire's residents became provincial M.L.A.'s. Early residents of the Eau Claire who followed their dream included R.B. Bennett, Peter Prince, Peter Turner-Bone, and James Lougheed.

Many Calgarians honed their dreams as they sat on the banks of the Bow River in Eau Claire.

Foxtails

Foxtails, those wispy, tickly but so awful tasting weeds. They were so good to caress and tickle with, but if you got them in your mouth the taste and feeling was terrible.

Back alleys and vacant lots were full of foxtails, but rarely would you see them in a garden or in grass.

At times, we would pull some stocks then sit on the back steps and just tickle our face or ears. The cat would come and play with them, but the dog did not like them on its face.

Sometimes, we would hold a friend and force foxtails in his mouth; yes, not a kind act. Even after you spit them out the stiff bristle like ends felt like they were still in your mouth. This plant could produce either agony or ecstasy, depending how it was used.

Frank Sinatra Jacket

A young singer named Frank Sinatra was exciting the youth through North America. One day there was a picture of him in the newspaper, and there was a description of the jacket he was wearing - the Frank Sinatra jacket.

There were not any for sale in Calgary, and if there were, we could not afford to buy one. However, unknown to me, my mother purchased some material from the short end box at Binnings, found some similar buttons, drew the pattern in my size, cut the material and proceeded to sew it together.

When my birthday came in May, much to my surprise was a magnificent Frank Sinatra jacket that fit just perfect. The sleeves, collar and pockets were of one material and the body of another cloth.

The next day, and for many days after that, I wore it to school. Later the jacket style was sold in the stores, but mine was probably the first one in Calgary.

Thanks, Mom!

Fun, Silliness, Badness or Hoodlums?

Many Eau Claire boys, living in small houses without the comforts and technological goods that were to change the behaviour patterns, were out playing on the streets. Was it all good mentally healthy play? No, not so. Unfortunately, those inconsiderate acts of childhood are like a 'monkey on your back' that can stay in your mind till time eternity.

With unpaved streets, there were always lots of rocks. The laundry windows, streetlights, windows of other homes, delivery wagons and on rare occasions, hobos and other children often became targets. In the latter case, it could mean the arrival of irate parents at the front door, a lecture and appropriate punishment. The breaking of a neighbourhood window would mean the arrival of the helmeted police in the black Maria, further lectures and "get the window paid for or else."

When the sun went down there was always the challenge of 'white rabbit', banging on doors or turning the ringing bells. It seemed that those homes where the occupants were so quick to come out and attempt to catch the culprits were those most bothered. Naturally, the gang would pressure someone to do the knocking while they hid behind protective coverage, trying not to giggle.

There were those who would bother the market gardeners, who sold their produce from their horse drawn wagons. There were several small hand laundries who suffered the inconsiderateness of boys throwing rocks or banging on their metal signs. Many homes had their gardens visited, and when the peas were ready to pick, it was probable that certain boys would taste from the vines.

Were these boys and girls any better or worse behaved than those of future generations? Certainly there was less profanity, perhaps more name calling, less animosity, but lots of silly and irritating mischief, now the 'monkey on your back'

Garbage Man

Our garbage man lived on 6A Street, with his large double garage directly behind but at a right angle to our back gate. The box on his truck was open to the wind.

Along the side of the back were compartments, which were used to store salvage. Besides collecting and hauling garbage for the city Mr. Brown and his partner were recyclers of the finest order.

Beer bottles, pop bottles, useable pieces of clothing, metal and wire were among the salvageable items. Each day, just past five, after the truck was returned home, the contents of the salvage boxes were removed and placed in the appropriate pile in the garage. About once a month, the insulated wire was burned in a barrel to recover the copper for resale.

Clothes and cloth were sold to a rag dealer, metal and wire went to a scrap dealer. Beer bottles, at 20 cents a dozen and pop bottles, 2 cents for small and a nickel for the large bottles were returned to the bottlers.

In many respects, recycling was also a way of life for many families in the Eau Claire. Clothes were passed down among the children of the family; neighbourhood boys searched the riverbanks each morning for beer bottles from the previous night's drinking sessions. Abandoned car seats were hauled into yards or up to porches to serve as a place to rest.

"Waste not, want not" was a philosophy generally practised on Eau Claire Avenue, with many items serving more than one person or family.

Garden Fairies

I peaked out the bedroom window, but my eyes were growing tired and the light was growing dim, but I had to see them.

Mom had told me about the garden fairies, and that they were only seen in the twilight as they used their magic wands to close the flower blossoms for the night.

I could see a dragonfly, some bees in the flowers and some sparrows along the fence, but where were the garden fairies? The light became dimmer as the sun dropped in the west and slipped behind a cloud. The corner street light came on, but still there were not any garden fairies in sight. My eyes grew tired, so I put my head on the old pillow and went off to sleep.

Gardens

More families than not, had a garden in their yard in the Eau Claire community. Besides being a hobby, they were a way of life and a necessity for many families just to feed themselves.

With our house at 711 being on a double lot, there was ample room on the east side to put in, what appeared through the eyes of a child, a large garden. The soil was rich, but being in the river valley, there were always rocks that worked their way to the surface. Closest to the front picket fence was the flower garden. Poppies, marigolds and sunflowers were found there, and these seemed to seed themselves. Rows of peas, beans, carrots, lettuce, onions and beets were planted in lines. Some years, corn was planted, but the season seemed too short to grow large cobs. Most of the garden space was given over to rows of potatoes. At the very south end were two small plots, outlined with boards, for the boy's gardens.

We had three wooden window boxes on the kitchen windows, and here, petunias were planted. On the eastside of the house, some chicken wire was the setting for the sweet peas.

Roses were not a flower to be generally found in the neighbourhood, but Parkins, on the corner, had borders of Californian poppies along their wire fence. At his house, around the corner, Mr. Gustafsen proved to be the botanical wizard of the neighbourhood, with his yard full of award winning dahlias. His raised and enclosed flowerbeds were roofed by a series of wires and cloth to control the light and moisture. He did not, however, leave any room in the yard for his children to play.

Yes, even at a very young age, it was my job to dig the garden in the spring, turning the soil over and pulling out the remains of dead vegetation. Summer meant pulling weeds, hilling the potatoes and watering. Sometimes potato bugs had to be removed. As the potato plants grew, they provided a setting for all sorts of creative play with cardboard houses, toy soldiers and models of farm animals,

The produce from our garden lasted well into the winter. Carrots were stored in boxes of sand in the cellar. Potatoes were bagged, and some of the vegetables were stored in glass sealers in the cool part of the cellar. The rubber rings used to seal the jars later were used in a ring toss game of accuracy.

One plant that formed part of our summer food supply was pigweeds, a spinach like plant that grew profusely in the alley. Some years we grew pumpkins and squash, but ours never seemed to reach the size of others in the neighbourhood.

Gardens were the basis of socialization as people worked in them in the evening and made contact with their neighbours over the fences.

Ghosts and Goblins at the Sawmill

Have you ever heard the sound of a circular saw cutting through logs? It builds up to a screech that to a small child can provoke images of strange creatures waiting in hiding to devour you.

Beside the large building that housed the sawmill machinery was a low dark structure that, through its narrow openings, you could see strange looking machinery, wires, and unknown apparatus. The water that flowed underneath seemed dark and mysterious. All of this was too scary to invite any of us to explore inside. Sometimes, as we peered inside, we thought that we could see monsters crouched here or there on the catwalks. The wind made strange sounds as it echoed through the structure, and cobwebs were strung among the beams.

Could there be snakes below the surface of the water; would there be poisonous spiders hanging from the cobwebs; was this the home of a wicked and deformed man that we often thought we saw following us through the bushes or in the sawmill yard as evening darkness was setting in?

Finally, one of the lumberjacks, who used to dance from log to log using his peavey pole to direct the logs to the mill, told us that the mysterious machinery had been used to make electricity for Calgary back in 'the old days'. He gently told us to stay away from the building because it was dangerous. He added as an afterthought,

"Don't forget, I told you to stay off the logs."

Ghosts in the Basement

I knew they were there! Had I seen them, no, not quite; had I heard them - maybe; had I smelled them, yes, I think so; but I could feel them; sometimes their touch was very, very close.

When the basement light was on, which was a single bulb hanging down from the cobwebbed ceiling; the ghosts could be hiding behind the piles of wooden and cardboard boxes that my mother kept. Sometimes I heard the ghosts in the coal room or under the dingy steps.

If someone was down in the basement with me the ghosts disappeared completely, but when I was there alone they managed to float in behind me. When I took my dog Sport downstairs, I watched him sniff around. He knew that ghosts had been there. They were the closest when I ran up the stairs and I knew they were right behind me, especially when I fumbled for the round light switch at the top of the stairs. When someone had closed the basement door, at the top of the stairs, the ghosts just about got me and I had to scream!

Grandparents

Pee Wee lived with his grandparents, Tommy lived two houses from his grandparents. There were others in Eau Claire that had grandparents in Calgary or out on the farm.

My dad's parents were in Scotland, which was about two weeks away by mail, and almost never by telephone, especially when you did not have one. One or two telegrams came, delivered to the house by a telegraph boy on his bicycle.

My grandmother at Cardston did not have a phone, or electricity for that matter. However, every summer, at least once, my father would load his old Essex, tie a couple of extra tires and tubes to the back, and with the six of us and the dog, head south. He drove up Cemetery Hill, past a few houses and then many farms on his way to Cardston. Part of the road was paved, but from Fort MacLeod, it was a dirt road that followed the road allowance. It was a long stretch without a store, almost without a house.

What a joy it was to arrive at the farm, give Grandmother a hug and get a drink of cool, fresh water.

Grandmother only came to visit us once at Eau Claire.

Graphics Arts Building

This two story red brick building, which covered the Sixth Street side of the block between First and Second Avenues was opened in 1912.

Many a time an Eau Claire child would stand at the large windows looking in on the Western Printing presses, watching the continual running of the printing machines being hand fed with sheets of paper at one end, dried by gas jets and the printed sheets removed at the other end.

By 1911 Western Printing, in partnership with the Herald, became the Herald-Western Co. Ltd. covering many aspects of printing and binding.

In the 1920's and 30's there was multi-colouring of posters, with the use of many metallic inks. Part of the workers contract was a daily supply of company financed milk to help the worker's body tolerate the metals that got on a worker's skin or in their lungs.

Washroom facilities were primitive in the print shop. One female employee found herself covered with bronze dust at the end of her shift. On another occasion a young woman had her long hair caught up in the rollers after another employee pushed a button too soon,

Paper for the presses came in wooden boxes. Youngsters in the Eau Claire area would 'borrow' the box tops to utilize in their clubhouse building.

On the second floor of the Graphic Arts Building were the offices of trade magazines, engravers and farm companies.

Grass Music

An activity learned from our older friends was to produce a shrill, ear splitting sound from a piece of quack grass.

A long piece of quack grass was placed taunt between the upper and lower joints of the thumbs. Then puckering up and blowing hard on the grass caused it to vibrate and produce the loudest and most hideous noise. Pleasant to anyone's ears, no, not even to our own, but it was creativity, even if not of musical quality.

Halloween

The night was alive with the shout of "Halloween apples." There were many children in Eau Claire so there was not a sense of loneliness that evening.

Who could afford store bought costumes and masks. Mom created ours, and, as often as not, it was a paper grocery bag with the eyes, nose, mouth and ears cut out. She encouraged us to decorate our own mask with crayons. We carried pillowcases or flour sacks to store our collection, which contained a good selection of apples.

We tried to work our way south of Fourth Avenue, because there were more affluent homes and hopefully a better treat.

I guess we tried to collect as many apples as Mom gave out, for we needed food for the table.

Most children looked after the other children. We just assumed the apples and treats were safe; parents allowed most children to have their own adventure, only to be bothered by the ghosts and goblins.

Hats

Everybody wore hats. Ladies wore a hat even if they went to the grocery store. Downtown there were ladies hat stores called millinery shops. Many girls, even women, wore tams.

Men wore hats. If you were a worker then a tweed hat with a front brim was the general attire. If you were a business or professional man, it was most often a fedora.

The postmen, milkmen or bread men all wore hats. The policeman wore a helmet. In the summer, some men wore straw hats. In the winter, there were fur hats, wool hats and/or earmuffs, with a curved piece of metal from one muff to the other.

What did boys wear? Most had a tweed hat, twisted and dirty from being pulled off your head and being flung around.

When I got my kilt suit from Scotland there was with it a black tam that had a silver Gordon Highlander's broach on the front of it. At first, it was too big, but a liner of newspaper helped. I was so proud of that hat that I wore it night and day. Other boys seemed to respect it too, and it was rarely pulled from my head to be tossed around. I believe it helped me to develop a little self~respect.

In the winter, boys liked to wear what was called an aviator's hat or helmet. They were often made of leather with a cloth or fleece lining, and long side flaps that could be snapped together under the chin.

A few boys had baseball hats, and I got one when I became a batboy for the Air Force team at Buffalo Stadium.

The Herald

As little money that my parents had, they still managed to put away 25 cents a week for the paper. Each day, Monday through Saturday, the Herald was delivered to our house between five and six p.m.

There were only two sections and the Saturday coloured comics. The headline was important as it gave us a quick look as to what the major concern of the day was. Without the sports, we would not know who won games in the six team National Hockey League. Frank McCool, who lived just across the street, was the goalie for the Toronto Maple Leafs. In the summer, where else could we get the baseball scores of the New York Yankees?

The Herald contained a social page describing who traveled to where or who attended whose tea party. Scary and mysterious were the goings on in Europe with Hitler or Stalin. Job listings in the classified were few and far between.

The Herald was used for more than reading. Poor people cut pages to fit in the sole of their shoes. In cold weather, sections of the paper were tucked under their sweater or jacket to act as insulation against the wind.

Many homes used newspaper beside the door to keep wet boots on. More than one home cut it into small sheets to keep beside the toilet.

Eau Claire boys folded its pages to make airplanes, flinging them into the air to make loop-the-loops. Newspaper was used for kites, but the paper ripped too easily and brown paper was better,

The Chinese vegetable man used newspaper to hold some of the produce he sold. The fish and chips shop on Centre Street gave you an order wrapped in newspaper.

Newspapers were used at the bottom of birdcages. Rabbit pens often had newspaper in them as bedding. Mom used crinkled newspaper to clean the top of our old black stove. Rarely did old newspaper end up in the garbage can.

Newspapers were often passed on to friends or neighbours who could not afford to purchase their own.

At the start of the war in 1939, and many times until it came to a close in 1945, there was the cry of "Extra, Extra," as newspaper sellers worked their way from the Herald Building to the Eau Claire with very special issues dealing with something of great importance.

Hide and Go Seek at the Sawmill

The sawmill yard was a great place to play hide and go seek. In addition to the fun of the game, there was also the risk of being caught inside the grounds by the guard.

As the location was further from our homes, we were able pursue this activity without the responsibility of younger siblings.

It was a dangerous place to play because boards could slip off the piles as you climbed them, and as well, slivers were numerous. However, there were many lumber stacks and piles of firewood and sawdust, not to mention wagons. There were more than enough places to hide and more than one way to slip home before you were caught.

There were times when a boy hid himself so well that he could not be caught, so the other players would quietly slip away and after a few minutes, the hidden player would find himself all alone in the scary lumberyard.

Highland Games

One of the sports highlights for some of us kids in Eau Claire was the annual Highland Games at Mewata Park.

Here we were in awe of the giants, at least to little kids, who threw the cabre, put the stone, threw the hammer and the 56-pound weight that we could hardly lift. We ran the track in our own little races; we stood behind the dancing platform and mimicked the dances of the Irish women. We gained inspiration from the skills of the competitors.

Back in the Eau Claire, we held our own Highland competitions.

Hitching a Ride on a Streetcar

There was one unwritten rule for the little kids in Eau Claire who wanted to be considered big kids, and that was to take an outside ride on the streetcar. Now this was dangerous and I had received several warnings from my parents, not to mention advice by my teacher as well as Mr. Richardson, the principal.

"Now, remember, it is dangerous to hang on to the back of a streetcar. Do not pull the cable of the electric line, and splitting tickets down the middle is dishonest."

For those who chose to hitch a ride, the summer was not the best time because you could not easily slide on the paving blocks. However, in the winter, the snow would be smooth and often icy.

I often watched the older boys hang on to the back of a streetcar and slide along the road. Many boots had hobnails on the soles and then the sparks would fly.

Finally, on cold, dark winter night, as the streetcar came to a stop on fourth Avenue, Eugene and I hung onto the back of the tram. It was dangerous but very exciting.

Just then, I heard my sister's voice, "Billy, I am going to tell Mom what you are doing." I let go and fell on my face. Then, catching my breath, I got up and ran home before my sister got there.

The Hobo Pack

Sometimes we went on a hike, perhaps along the railroad tracks to Lawry gardens and once even as far as Brickburn. A lunch was necessary, and this would generally consist of a jam sandwich, an apple and Dad's cookies. To be a hobo we needed a hobo's pack. This was accomplished by going in Mom's rag bag, finding a cloth, putting our food in, tying the four corners together and inserting a carrying stick through the tie. All done! I would put the stick over my shoulder and off we would go.

Hobo Village

One Saturday, my father cranked up the car and invited me to go for a ride. We drove up Sixth Street to Ninth Avenue and headed East, past the massive Palliser Hotel, the train station and the freight sheds, then turned north and parked by the River.

"I am going to show you 'Hobo Village' , and then you will see how lucky we are to have a roof over our heads."

Here, in this field, which my father had said was the station lands for an old railroad company, were groups of men, some boiling water or cooking food over fires, others washing or shaving using pans of water, others lying on a bedroll, watching us as we walked by to see if we had brought any food to hand out.

There were a few tents and pieces of canvas strung up to provide some protection from the sun or rain.

My father carried a paper bag in his hand. As we approached an elderly man sitting with a tattered blanket over his shoulders his face broke into a smile when he recognized my father. "Here is a sandwich and an orange for you, Charlie, and this is my son Billy."

We soon left the area and drove home. I was so thankful to be able to go in and turn on the kitchen tap and have an electric light over the kitchen table.

Hoboes

Gaunt faces and stubble on their cheeks, baggy patched clothes and hat held in hand; victims of the depression or of their own shortcomings, these men often made a round of the block asking at each door, "Any work I can do for a sandwich?'

Some doors were closed in their faces; other times a polite no, but sometimes there was weed pulling or sweeping to be done.

Sometimes Mom would make a jam sandwich, or if the potatoes were on to boil a hot slice of one on the end of a fork would be handed out.

I suppose Eau Claire saw more of these homeless and hungry men because we were close to the river where they could find a place to rest or even sleep at night.

Was there a name that could be applied to them? I guess at the time, and at that place, Hobo was the term used. What history needs are their written stories.

Hockey Games at Victoria Arena

As I grew older and realized that Calgary extended south beyond the railway tracks, I became familiar with the huge and exciting Victoria Arena, located just about where the Saddledome now sits.

With permission from my parents, I would catch the streetcar on Fourth Avenue, transfer downtown to a Number 5, Beltline, and travel to Seventeenth Avenue East. This was done an hour or more before the game because we had to face standing in line for a rush seat. Where were they located, well right along the rink boards, almost on the ice, and without the benefit of safety wire, which was only behind the goal. We sat or kneeled on the bench as close to the play as you could get.

There was not much opportunity to leave your seat between periods, because there was always someone behind you to fill it. Your time was spent watching the rink rats pulling the barrels with canvas attached to spread the water and flood the ice.

If you remembered, you had put a jam sandwich in your pocket for who had money for hotdogs.

Later, thanks to the Cross family and the Calgary Buffalo Association, I got to play many games, some with players who went on to the National Hockey League, in the old Victoria Arena.

Homemade Root Beer

"Don't sell any beer bottles, Billy. We are going to make root beer next week."

Good! Mom's root beer was good. It was almost like magic that she could make root beer at home.

Next week my sisters washed the bottles; Mom mixed the ingredients and filled the bottles. Dad put the caps on.

When they were all finished the bottles were stacked in one of the bedrooms and a blanket put over them to, I think, keep the light out and the heat in. With luck, none of the bottles would explode and they had to be left alone for at least a week.

A few days later, we heard a 'pop' as one of the corked bottles had built up enough pressure to blow its top. Fortunately, this was the only accident, and a few days later, we were able to enjoy the taste of our labours.

Horses

The smell and sounds of horses permeated the Eau Claire area. First and foremost was Teddy, our Shetland pony. If it was not in the yard, we kept it tethered in the field that was later to become Buffalo Stadium.

I rode Teddy in the Stampede parades. My Costume was cowboy; while my brother Bobby, on a borrowed pony, was dressed in an Indian outfit, my mother had made out of burlap potatoe bags.

One fall day I rode Teddy to McDougall School, which was about four blocks away. I tied the horse to the fence and went to my grade three room. However, Mr. Richardson, the principal, came to visit me and suggested I take Teddy home at noon and leave him there.

There were other horses stabled in the Eau Claire area. On First avenue, just a canter away, was the stable and wagon yard for the Producer's Dairy, which was located on Third Avenue and Fifth Street. The dairy's huge Clydesdale and Percheron horses pulled the milk wagons daily on their routes around the city. Sometimes, on a warm evening, the horseman would lead them down to the Bow to drink and cool off in the water.

The Union Milk, Model and Co-op Dairy wagons made their rounds in the Eau Claire district, and as well, the McGavin and Four X bakery wagons. In season, we had theChinese produce wagons and the Alberta Ice Company wagon.

On occasion a scrap or rag dealer might show up to solicit goods of that nature.

On a hot day, children would follow the ice wagon on its rounds in the hope of getting a small chunk of ice to cool their mouths. In retrospect, the market garden horse and wagon were not treated so kindly as a well-placed rock would cause the Chinaman's horse to take off down the street, back door of the wagon swinging open and produce falling on the street.

Horseshoes

Clank, clank; the familiar sound of horseshoes being pitched on a summer evening or weekend. Several yards in our block and vacant lots had horse pits, the lengths of which varied with the size of the available space in the yard or lot. Generally, Sunday mornings were quiet as this activity was frowned upon in many households on the Sabbath.

Sometimes a pair of players from a street or so over would walk to Eau Claire for a match, sometimes with a side bet. Once in a while there was a howl or a swear as a heavy metal shoe did not catch in the sand and bounced or slid to catch one of the players in the shin.

With several stables in the Eau Claire area, there were good sources for horseshoes, but those that had been worn by the workhorses were extra heavy.

Many local residents had, for luck, a horseshoe attached to the gate or above the door.

Hot Cross Buns

Oh, that beautiful smell again; Mom has been baking.

"One a penny, two a penny, hot cross buns."

"Mom, may we have a hot cross bun with jam?"

"Wash your hands Billy; how you can get so dirty is beyond me. Try to use a little soap and don't forget the water."

I washed and scrubbed then used the towel to dry.

Funny, it seemed that all of our kitchen towels were worn and had a hole in the middle.

Mom gave me a delicious hot bun, which made me want another. However, I had to wait for supper to get a second.

The Ice Wagon

"Billy, hurry up, the ice wagon is coming down the street." It was a very hot July day and how nice it would be to have a piece of ice to suck on, even if there were crumbs of sawdust stuck to it.

The wagon stopped and the driver came to the back of the wagon, opened the doors, picked his tongs, and lifted out a large piece of ice to deliver next door.

"Now you kids stay away from the ice, hear me?"

"Yes Sir," we replied, but as soon as he left, we reached in over the cold damp floor to reach the broken pieces of cold, clear ice.

When the iceman had finished several deliveries to the more affluent families of the block, he came back to the wagon and said, "All right boys, you can now get a piece of ice." Gladly did we retrieve our third or fourth piece of ice?

Once in a while, when my parents had an extra 25 cents, the iceman would deliver a block of ice for our icebox.

Sometimes in the winter, we would go with our father to the river and chop pails of ice, which we would pull back on the sleigh. It would be stored in a cold storage box that was buried in the ground in the front yard. There were some households in Eau Claire that had root cellars. Here many blocks of ice could be stored and insulated with sawdust from the Eau Claire lumber mill.

Icicles

"Dad, will you get us down some icicles?"

"Yes, Billy, but don't suck on them, and if you are fencing watch out for your eyes. The ice is sharp and dangerous."

Our sloped kitchen roof was a great place for icicles to grow. The sun melted the snow and the water dripped over the edge to form long columns of ice.

Foe against foe; dancing, darting; careful not to have your ice shaft snapped or broken by your opponent before you scored a 'body touch', which made you the winner. More often than not, the ice swords would clash and both would be broken, and so would the rules with the dueller with the longest piece of ice remaining, claiming to be the winner.

Sometimes the short pieces could be hidden behind your back and then slid down the collar of your friend's shirt when he was looking the other way.

Other times we wandered the neighbourhood to find those gigantic icicles that could be broken off with a stick or broom handle. We had to be so careful that a massive chunk of ice would not fall down on us.

The Icing Bowl

"Billy, do you want to lick the icing bowl?" What wonderful words to hear. I didn't even know that Mom had baked a cake. With her pans, she would bake two round cakes, put icing in between and then cover the top. With the icing bowl, and cake for supper I would be double lucky.

Actually, the licking was more so of the spoon that I would use to scrape every bit of the vanilla or chocolate icing from the bowl. It was best to scrape a little icing, then let it sit in your mouth so that you had that wonderful taste, scrape a little more and not really rush the complete removal of that delicious icing made by my mother. How lucky I was to have an understanding, Mom.

Jam Can Curling

There were not any curling rinks in the Eau Claire area, but most of us had seen it played on the ice beside the Victoria Arena. There were times we curled with river rocks on the ice of the river, but to develop a game this way was not easy.

One day, Tommy's mom told us about jam can curling. We listened to her, and then knocked on a few doors to gather our needed eight jam pails. With this accomplished, we filled them half full of water, put a piece of lath wood in to serve as a handle and left them out in the yard to freeze. The next day, we used a crayon to colour the handles, yellow and red.

Now, for a rink. We had been warned to stay away from the river, so we decided on a flat space beside the house where the kitchen drain pipe had caused some ice to form.

We packed snow and hauled out pails of water and two days later, we had a sheet of ice. Crayons again faintly marked the points to aim for.

We only had two teams of three, so it was decided to let the captains throw the first can and the last.

It took a few shots to develop enough force on the cans without tipping them over. We decided that a tipped can was out of play.

We played for several days until a heavy snow and cold weather kept us indoors. Later, after we had cleaned and lengthened the ice, we were able to play some more games.

The Jimmy Allen Club

Located on the corner of Fourth Street and Fifth Avenue was a British American (BA) Service Station. This station was revered by many Eau Claire children because British American sponsored the Jimmy Allen Club.

Jimmy Allen was a pilot, real or otherwise. When you joined his club you received a membership card, small wings to wear on your shirt or jacket and printed aviation material. A sense of belonging, something free and a zest for flying machines drew many of us to join.

Naturally those children whose fathers owned automobiles, and there were not that many, would plead and direct the driver to a BA station.

Kaleidoscope

One Christmas I received a kaleidoscope. I had never seen one before, and as I unwrapped it, I thought it was a telescope, just as Captain Hook used on his pirate ship.

However, as I put my eye to the peek hole I realized that what I would see inside was a mystery. As I turned the end, the coloured pictures and shapes continually changed to form new patterns. How could this happen, how many different designs could I make, how could I be so lucky to get such a marvellous present for Christmas?

I enjoyed it; my brother and sisters had to have their turn with this magical viewer, and my friends were equally impressed.

The King is Coming!

The King is coming, the King is coming! Hurrah, we get a holiday! This was the shout heard through the McDougall School playground that sunny fall day in 1937.

As part of a cross-Canada tour, the Royal Couple were to be driven through Calgary streets in an open automobile.

Our teacher talked to us about the British Empire and the Royal Family. We drew Union Jacks and located England and London on our wall map.

Finally, the day to see the Royal Family came, and, although we did not get a holiday, we were marched, as a class, along Fourth Avenue to a spot just west of Louise Bridge. Here each student was given a small flag to wave.

We stood for a long while, waiting for this momentous occasion. My mother had given me a vanilla bottle that she had filled with homemade lemonade, and this I drank when I got thirsty.

Finally, a long black open car, the likes of which I had never seen before, came into view - and was past so fast that, if you would have winked, you would have missed it.

A Long Train Trip

My father joined the Air Force after war was declared in the fall of 1939. He was sent to St. Thomas, Ontario, for training. One day after school, my mother informed me that we would be going there also. Next day at school, I looked at the Canada map and realized that St. Thomas was a long, long way away.

Our rented house was re-rented, furniture and all. My two sisters went to live with an aunt. The clothes and necessary needs of my mother, my brother and me were squeezed into two old suitcases. Mom also carried a bag of food, pillow and a blanket for our three day train journey east.

My aunt drove us to the train station to board the train. We could not afford a sleeper, but we managed to get two seats that faced each other. At the end of the coach was a coal burning stove that soup or food could be heated on. As well, there were food sellers that went through the train with sandwiches, fruit and drinks.

It was a long, uncomfortable journey, across the prairies and through the forests of Northern Ontario. We arrived in Toronto tired and dirty, but then it was just a short train ride to St. Thomas. Here my father had rented a room and a hallway where my brother and I slept.

Was the trip fun, no, but as an adventure it was first rate.

Looking Through the Ice

"Billy, where are you going?"

"Oh, just out Ma."

"Don't go near the river; do not go out on the ice."

Off I went, and often to the river. It was interesting to see if the river had overflowed and there was new shiny ice downstream from the hole. Also interesting was the ice that was clear, which allowed you to look through it and see the water flowing below, other levels of ice and of the rocks on the riverbed.

Try as I might to see a fish swim by, it did not happen. However, if the ice was clear under the weir one could see a school of suckerfish that lived there.

Sometimes the new ice could be used for a game of kid's curling. If we could find rocks that were not frozen solid we would slide them on the ice to see who could come the closest to a stick stuck through the ice. Any number of boys could play and there was not a limit to the number of rocks that one could throw. Often an argument would develop as to whose rock was whose. Then we discovered that if we carried some crayons with us that we could mark our ownership. However, that brought about further arguments as to who got which colour. Boys, being boys, we had our favourite colour and there were colours that we did not like.

Maggots

Maggots, those wiggly little garbage produced creatures. However, at times, we made a penny or two from them. There were always fishermen on the river and they found the maggots good bait. We would, after locating a nest, scoop them into an Eddie Match box or a small tin.

Sometimes on the way to the river we might scare some girls with the maggots, but not if the girls had a big brother. Some fishermen would buy, some would not. There were those that did not have a penny to spare.

If we did not sell them, we might take them to one of the numerous pools where we knew the fish hung out, dropping them into the water and watch the fish rise to eat them.

Making Airplanes

Calgary's skies were often buzzing with single propeller double wing flying machines known as biplanes that did loop-the-loops, dives and other devious manoeuvres.

With the advent of the war and the pilot training at No. 3 Flying Training School, located south of the Currie Army Barracks, there was a succession of Harvard and Anson training planes continually flying over Calgary.

Mentioned elsewhere is the Jimmy Allen Flying Club for children, that was sponsored by British American gasoline. This, the war, and the multitude of planes over Calgary, gave boys, and girls also, the encouragement to build and fly model airplanes.

There were those crude models, made with a flat piece of wood nailed to a round piece of wood, got from the river. Sometimes a father or big brother would carve a simple propeller that would be attached to the nose, and, as you ran, the propeller might or might not turn.

We made paper airplanes by the dozen; a sheet of paper folded double to make the wings, another piece of paper folded twice to form the body and inserted into the wings, fold the nose over to hold the body in, and draw a design on the wings.

Many backyard competitions were held to see if we could make the planes do a manoeuvre or whose creation could glide the furthest.

The greatest accomplishment, and also the source of great frustration, was the construction of balsam wood models that were powered by a windup elastic band that powered the propeller.

Hours could be spent using one of Father's old razor blades to cut out the numbered pieces from a sheet of balsam wood that was part of the plane kit. These kits cost from 10 to 35 cents. Care and concern was needed to cut the small pieces accurately, and there was despair and frustration when a slip was made. Sometimes the pieces turned red from the blood of a cut finger.

Further frustration could result when you glued the pieces together and glue joined the wood to your fingers.

Finally, the frame model was put together and the propeller and the power elastic added. You had to be careful not to wind too tight because a poorly built model might then bend in the middle.

A well-built model brought about a sense of pride, but then there was the decision to fly it or to hang it by thread from the bedroom ceiling.

A Marble Tournament

"Billy, do you want to go to a championship marble tournament tomorrow? It's over in Riverside, but do not bring your best shooters because these guys are pros and you will lose them."

The next morning we took the streetcar downtown, got a transfer, and then got on the Bridgeland tram, getting off just over the bridge and then it was just a short walk to the vacant land beside the Alberta Ice Company.

There were several games already in progress; players and spectators alike, talking, laughing, groaning as shots were missed, and others offered encouragement to players.

The rings were massive, which meant that it would be much more difficult to make an accurate shot. However, the challenge of playing in Calgary's 'master' marble tournament was worth the risk. We got an invite to play from two boys that we did not know.

"Do you guys want a game, five marbles in the ring, no cracked or chipped marble allowed? Any hunching and you add two marbles. If your shooter stays in the ring you add another marble, okay?"

A three foot ring was dropped in the dirt, twenty marbles, five each, were dropped in the ring and the game began. Our opponents claimed first shots and they cleaned out eight marbles before we even had a shot. My first shot went clean through the circle. However, after that I settled down and knocked three marbles out.

I had brought about twenty marbles, but I had lost them all except my lucky shooter in about ten games.

Afterwards we watched the 'masters' in action, listened to their good luck chants, made new friends and promised to come back next week.

Closer to home, games were played near the fire escapes at McDougall School where the dirt was generally free of the furnace cinders that were spread in the schoolyard.

Another place that saw many marble games was in the yard of the dairy barns on First Avenue.

Marbles

There were many a game of marbles played in the Eau Claire. Any place that the dirt was firm and a circle could be drawn in it a marble game could be held. The McDougall School fields were covered with cinders from the school furnace, so there were only small areas where the game could be played, but there were many vacant lots in the neighbourhood, as well, back yards and the dairy stable yard were put to use.

Sometimes games were interrupted by an irate mother who came to retrieve a son who was overdue at home for chores or supper.

Some boys had their own leather or cloth bag to hold their marbles. Some of us only had our pockets. Although the game was called marbles, we would often call individual pieces agates.

Eau Claire's marble facilities and competition was secondary to that which took place on weekends in front of the Alberta Ice stables in Riverside. Here the better players gathered to compete, while those of lesser ability watched,

Play was often supervised by Hunis, the 'Riverside Sheriff', a local man who wore suspenders with the word 'Sheriff' printed on the clasps. As well, Hunis had a great sense of humour. Perhaps from situations such as this comes the term, "He has lost his marbles."

Matinees

Saturday afternoon matinee movies were generally the centre of a child's entertainment during the 'old days'. Motion pictures at school were extremely rare and, of course, there was not any television.

Almost all theatres had matinees. For the kids from Eau Claire there were many theatres and films to choose from. Across Louise Bridge was the Plaza; downtown the Capital and Palace were awesome structures to the kids from the tenements and frame houses of Eau Claire. Their architecture, ceilings and moulding seemed more in character to the metropolitan cities of the world. The Grand, on First Street West, contained a long ramp that took you up to its balcony, where it seemed that you were looking almost straight down on the stage. Further South, across the tracks, was the Isis, which, it seemed, had six rows across and fifty rows deep, not quite, but it seemed that way when you were 'just a kid'

On Eighth Avenue the Regent and Bijou were not in operation by the time, I was old enough to go, however the Strand and the Variety, even if their projectors jerked and dissolved the film, offered the most entertainment for the price. Serials, cartoons, westerns, stage entertainment and giveaways were often included in the price of admission.

There was the Ghost of the Hitching Post as well as many other small theatres that we would hear about, but would never see the silent films that they had shown. Matinees often had two or three cartoons, often Castle films, in black and white. The main feature would often be an adventure serial, cowboy or otherwise, in three or more parts, ending at an exciting moment with enough mystery to draw you back the next Saturday.

Cost - normally ten cents, but sometimes as low as a nickel. Boys and girls would line up long before the doors opened. Sometimes there was the added incentive of a small prize for each ticket holder. For adults some theatres held a dish night when a free dish, cup or saucer brought the ladies in.

Balconies were set aside for the smokers. If a parent brought a son or daughter to the matinee that is where the children experienced second-hand smoke.

The Maypole

McDougall School had a Maypole, and each spring the teachers would place it in the gym so that the classes could begin practising on it.

Our Maypole had been made many years before, but because of the wear and tear on the streamers, it had to be repaired each winter. Mothers of the Home and School Association would cut and dye strips of cotton sheets. With all of the repetitions of pulling and bending, the strips did well to hold up.

Every student took place in the practises that were held several times a week. It was a serious matter and even the worst troublemakers or silliest boys upheld the honour of their class by learning the dance pattern quickly and thoroughly. Only about twelve students at a time would be part of the group that pranced and wove the streamers in the colourful and complex ceremony that honoured the Roman goddess of flowers.

McDougall School

If Egypt had the pyramids and New York had the Empire State Building, then Eau Claire had McDougall School, even if it was across Fourth Avenue.

I went to McDougall from Grade one through grade nine. Any type of schooling before grade one was unknown in the Eau Claire. No, I did not fail grade one, but Eugene did and then he was just recommended for the rest of his schooling.

McDougall was a wonderful place to gather.each day. The girl's entrance was on the north side and the boys on the south side. The School Board offices were on the east side, with the walkway to their door fenced off and lined with flowers. Around much of the schoolyard were fir trees and a fence made of pipe. There were three playing areas, girl's and boy's fields on the east side and the large soccer and baseball field to the west. This area was rough on bare legs as the cinders from the furnace were spread out here.

Before the bell was rung, we were not allowed into the school except in very cold or rainy weather. At nine and one-thirty, the vice principal would come out and ring his hand bell. The school was built of sandstone, and we would take the hook on a chain that held the door open and carve into the soft stone. There were places where someone in the past had carved initials into the stone.

In the basement were the manual training room, large washrooms for boys and girls, two large playrooms with benches along each wall, the wood room and the furnace room.

The school was the most beautiful building in Eau Claire. There were wide stairs at each end of the building, spacious hallways, beautiful doors and wood panelling and four hanging lights in each classroom. Each classroom had a cloakroom with two rows of metal coat hooks. The cloakroom was also used to put bad boys in. Each floor had boys and girls washrooms and there was a nurse's room on the second floor.

The gym, with a stage, was in the middle of the third floor. On the fourth floor was a small museum and the janitor's quarters. A metal fire escape provided a safe way down from each floor and a practise fire drill was held each month.

Being a student at McDougall gave us a sense of pride that carried through into adult life.

McDougall School Museum

The top floor of McDougal School was a place of mystery for me and probably most students. We knew that the janitor lived up there. He would be yelling at you from the top of the fire escape if you did something that was frowned upon when you played on the grounds during the evening or the weekend.

One day our teacher told us that we had a special treat and that she would take us to 'the museum'. This was great, for museum was a magical word for us, bringing to mind a distant city where the mysteries of Greece or Egypt might be found.

Finally, after we were lined up, we were marched up to the fourth floor, our first time visit here. Yes, there was a museum, no statues or mummies from another time, but many stuffed birds and animals, bird eggs, bird and animal skeletons and fossils set in stone. This display had been housed on the fourth floor of McDougall School for many years, but we did not know that. I wonder where it is today?

Milkman's Helper

With the dairy's stables just a block away, and the dairy itself not much further, there were many opportunities to be a milkman's helper.

We knew most of the horses and often helped to feed them, hose them down and use a currycomb on their manes.

The milk wagons had steps on the back, which we often rode. Along each side of the wagon's central aisle were compartments for the milk and dairy products. Ice helped to keep the goods cool in the summer, and a blanket helped to keep the goods from freezing in the winter.

Milk was bottled in glass quart bottles, with the cream rising to the top. The hardboard cap could rise as much as two inches in frigid weather as the milk froze and expanded.

The milkmen who delivered in the Eau Claire area would let us hold the reins and attempt to make the mouth noises to start and stop the horse. However, these horses knew their routes, where to stop and when to start, so the driving was just a formality.

Sometimes we were allowed to carry a quart of milk to the door, remembering to bring back an empty bottle and a token or milk ticket.

Mom's Canary

Mom had a yellow canary; it seemed as if she had always had a canary. It was our alarm clock in the morning, especially on those sunny days of summer.

The cage hung on a hook over a kitchen window. There was a time when it was over the kitchen table, but too much birdseed found its way into the food.

Once a week my father would clean out the birdcage and cut out a piece of newspaper to fit on the floor. The water and birdseed dishes had to be cleaned out. Sometimes a piece of apple or vegetable would be jammed between the cage wires.

Mom would talk to 'Dickie" much of the time she was in the kitchen, using both words and whistles. Sometimes, in the evening, my father would shut the door and let the canary out of its cage. However, the bird seemed more frightened than happy with this freedom. Dad would turn out the light and then it was easier to capture the bird.

We had several canaries and they were all named 'Dickie'

Mourning Armbands

Few men, unless they were in work clothes, would venture downtown in other than a suit, tie and hat.

Another piece of apparel worn by some was a dark armband fastened to the upper arm of a jacket or coat. The purpose of this was to show respect or acknowledgement that a relative of the wearer had died. Depending upon the closeness of the deceased person, these mourning armbands could be worn for months.

Death is often a mystery to small boys, but if we were aware of the armband, all silliness and giggling stopped until we were long past the person wearing it.

The Move to 711

Before 711, the family had lived in the front side of a duplex on Second Avenue. Little, if any, do I remember of the time there.

However, impressed on my mind was the move to 711 Eau Claire. My father had borrowed a truck with a flatbed on the back and solid rubber tires, which I knew were different than our car tires.

I stood holding my teddy bear, which had no arms or legs but was nevertheless mine, and watched my parents load beds, chairs, tables and a gramophone onto the truck. My father sat me on the front seat and off we drove to the new house. It seemed like a long way, but I was to later realize that it was only three blocks.

The house looked big with its second floor, and the yard was so much larger than our old house.

My dad took me around back and showed me the sandbox, the first I had ever seen or played in. For some strange reason I buried my armless friend in the sand. Perhaps in my mind this was the start of a new life in a new house.

Mud Puddle Navy

Eau Claire Avenue, in the Six Hundred block, was not paved, and in spots where some effort had been made there were bits of green boulevard. With the road cresting, there was good drainage to each side here and there, and during a rainstorm, wonderful puddles were created. With the lay of the road, the edges were irregular, and for a child with a good imagination these puddles were the seas and oceans of the world.

On rare occasion, a child might be the owner of a store bought boat, painted and regent in design. However, for the most part, the boats or ships were a flat piece of wood, sawed to form a bow, with smaller pieces of wood or thread spools nailed on top to form the superstructure. If it were to be a warship shingle nails mounted at the front or back served as the guns.

Sometimes there would be a sailboat, one mast with an old hankie or piece of a flour sack used to make a sail. If there were not any small nails available to tack the sail down then old, gramophone needles served the purpose.

In late summer, pea boats made their appearance. Take a good fat pea pod, split it carefully along the top, eat the peas and use a half a matchstick to hold the pod open.

On a puddle that flowed towards a drain, races could be held. This worked well for the larger boats, but the pea boats sometimes slipped through the grate.

Where did the water go when it went down the drain? For the young mind, there was mystery and mystique, with the thought of monsters and water snakes.

Mud puddles created urges in little boys to push other boys or girls in to create wet shoes and socks. When puddles froze, they were a good place to slide.

In hot weather, the dogs liked to sit or lie in the puddles to cool off. The puddle was a source of drinking water to animals and birds.

Muffs

Did your mother wear a muff; mine did. It was a grey fur tube like piece of clothing that had a small purse on the top and openings at each end in which to place your hands to keep them warm. The fur matched my mother's coat, one that she had purchased at a church rummage sale. There were times when I came in from outside, fingers red and cold, and I would put my hands in the muff to help take away the stinging pain.

Mumble - The - Peg

There was a game that the bigger boys played called 'mumble-the peg' . The game revolved around the skills of throwing a knife into the ground so that it stuck in.

First, a circle would be drawn on the ground. Then, whoever was first,would throw their opened pocketknife into the circle and, if it stuck in, it would mark the division of the circle. The other player would then throw to cut the property even further. This would continue until the slice of the circle could not be cut any further, then the last cutter was the winner.

Make sense, not totally, however, it did give the participants an opportunity to practise their knife skills.

Because of the knowledge to the obvious dangers, many parents were very reluctant to allow their son to possess a knife. However, a boy's need to assert himself has always been part of the maturing process.

However, knives had many other uses. There were lots of willow by the river and the wood was good for miniature carvings. We sharpened our arrows and carved initials in trees and fences. A pile of discarded soapstones was found in the Eau Claire and the boys carved the figures of animals and people from this soft stone.

My Favourite Cafes

Little boys were expected to stay close to home, but some, more than others, have a strong desire to see what is around the next corner, to just go another block, or to explore Calgary's downtown. The latter was more inviting if you had a coin or two in your pocket.

On Eighth Avenue and Fifth Street was the Wave. Here if you purchased a pop you could read comic books for an hour. A block further east was Polus's Puss and Boots, a regular café with a 'u' shaped counter with seats that had spinning tops.

Peter, as son, went to McDougall School, so there were times when his Greek father supplied a treat to his son's friends.

Across the avenue was a unique café that was housed in an old railroad passenger car, minus the wheels. Prices were higher; children were not as welcome without their parents, especially those without money to spend.

Further east, Picardys had the best pastry, if you could afford it. The White Lunch Cafeteria served pancakes for ten cents all day long. The Bus Depot café, in the Greyhound building, was always a hive of activity of people coming and going.

On the way home, we would press our noses against the floor to ceiling windows of the Tea Kettle Inn on Seventh Avenue. Here well-dressed ladies sat sipping their tea and eating off fine china on linen tablecloths. They were served by waitresses with lace collar and tiny hats.

My Favourite Yard

It would be hard to count the number of times I had walked by the exciting and colourful yard on Second Avenue that was full of birdhouses, windmills, whirlybirds, animated scenes and folk art projects.

The house was immaculate, the yard and gardens pristine yet I never did see anyone working in the yard. Perhaps the care was done early in the morning or late evening, past my bedtime.

Many of the beautifully carved and painted birdhouses sat on top of poles placed in the ground. Some were placed or hung from a tree, and here and there was a statuary collections of folk art.

It was not the biggest or grandest yard in Eau Claire, but it was a pleasure and an inspiration to a small boy.

My First Goal

In the life of any boy, the first hit in baseball, the first one-handed catch, the first length of the pool, the first strike in bowling, or the first goal in soccer may often be an accomplishment that is long remembered.

Soccer was a daily noon activity at McDougall School. The soccer field was covered with ashes from the school's coal burning furnace, With a lunch break that was an hour and a half long, we could end up with fifty boys chasing the beat up soccer ball, hoping to get a least one kick at it.

One day in early September, Mr. McRae announced that McDougall would have two soccer teams, a junior and a senior, to play games against other schools. We held practises and then the team was picked; I had made substitute! That was okay because most of the juniors were a year older than me and certainly bigger. In fact, I was the smallest boy on the team.

Sunnyside School came to our field to play us. The ball was kicked back and forth, and then Sunnyside scored just before the first half ended. I hadn't played, but I was there and wore one of McDougall's shirts.

Mr. McRae gave encouragement to the players, and then he said, "Billy, go in as left forward." My system was shocked, but I knew I could run with the other players.

I managed to kick the ball twice, but then I missed it on an easy pass. Then towards the end of the game, Stan had a corner kick. I stood in front of their goal, being guarded by a much bigger boy who tried to push me away.

Stan kicked the ball, a high, long kick that dropped down in front of me. Without thinking, and probably with eyes closed, I swung my left foot at the ball, Bang!, and it went between the posts!

The game ended with a one - one score, and I had gotten our goal. My first goal!

The Mystery House

Across the alley, surrounded by many trees and a sturdy fence, was the local house of mystery. Not only did it appear to be dark and sinister, but also the two elderly occupants spoke what appeared to little children such as us, a strange dialect.

However, in later years, on second sight, the house was gracious; the grounds were immaculate and prolific of plant life. The two polite and gracious people spoke French to themselves, and by then we had matured and were less provincial.

New Year's Party

"If you can behave yourself, Billy, you can come over to Mr. Hunter's 'Hogmanay' (New Year's Party). Now put on a clean shirt, wash your face, brush your hair and leave the dog at home, Sport will sit on their porch and howl until you come out.

I was so very happy, for I was being allowed to stay up late and go to a New Year's party.

After brushing my boots and brushing my hair, being careful not to use the same brush for both, I fastened Sport to the rope on the doghouse. "No Sport, dad says you cannot come," although 'cannot' came out as 'canna' as my father would say in his Scottish manner.

I ran out the gate, down the sidewalk, around the corner and in the Hunter's back gate. I could hear my father's accordion and singing coming from the basement where the party was taking place.

I peaked into the kitchen and on the counter were more beer and whiskey bottles than I had ever seen in my life. What magic did these bottles contain that brought out such silliness and laughter in older people?

I reached up and grasped a tall, greenish bottle, and, as the lid was off, put the bottle to my lips and carefully took a drink.

My tongue felt as if it were floating in a thousand tiny bubbles, and as the liquid trickled into my stomach it did feel like magic! I took another drink and then another. I felt wonderful! Just then, my father, who had come up from the basement, spoke, "Billy, you have drunk enough of Mrs. Hunter's ginger ale; time for you to go home."

Nicknames

Much, to many parents dismay, most children soon earned nicknames, generally given to them by playmates and friends. Sometimes children created their own nickname, perhaps to draw attention to themselves, perhaps in defiance of their parents, or perhaps because of teasing about their own name. Whatever the reason nicknames abounded.

Fuzzy, Curly, Scottie, Lefty, Snooky, Willie - all nicknames at one time or another. Fuzzy and curly I did not like because I did not like my curly hair. Playing baseball, Lefty was great; Snooky came about because I was always snooping into everything.

Names seemed to go with generations. James, Charles, Robert, William and Jack were the most common male names.

It seemed that if you had a one-syllable name your chances of having a nickname were lessened. Yet it seemed so much easier to remember a person by their nickname.

I still remember my friend Robert, who lived across the street, as Bud or Buddy. Arthur, on the corner, was, and still is, Pee Wee. Stan was Sunny, and Dennis was Sharky. Jack, with his red hair, naturally went by Red.

Nationality played a major role in nicknames. Scottie, Mick, Frenchie, Swede and many other names were used, but these were generally made to friends in a compatible way.

Teachers were often referred to as 'old man' or 'old lady' someone, but then these prefixes could be applied to anyone over thirty. Policemen, in their helmet shaped hats, were often called 'flatfoots', homeless men were called tramps. That doesn't mean you would not go into the kitchen and bring them out something to eat.

So much of the name-calling was done in a spirit or camaraderie, a sharing of something personal.

The Noon Hour Whistle

The noon hour whistle! What a joy it was to the ears of the many women who toiled in the heat and noise of the Alberta and Premier Laundries, not to mention the pupils of McDougall School. Several blocks away the noon whistle of the Eau Claire sawmill brought men and their peavey poles off the river while others shut down the saw and log conveyor.

An hour of rest for fatigued muscles - an hour of relief from the heat and humidity of the wash tubs, mangles and irons - an hour of rest from the screeching saw, carrying and piling lumber, or just knowing that the foreman had his eye on you.

Girls and women streamed home to the small one or two room apartments in the area that they called home. Often a butter box fastened to the wall outside a window served as a fridge, and dishes were washed in a common bathroom. A quick and simple lunch and hopefully a few minutes rest on a dilapidated Winnipeg couch that served both as a sofa and a bed.

The men at the sawmill carried their tin lunch pails and flopped down in the shade of a pile of lumber. What a relief to rest, particularly after an evening of drinking red eye at the Victoria Hotel.

The noon hour whistle was a reminder to the principal to ring the dismissal bell if he had not already done so. If it was summer and children were spread every which way it was a reminder, in the days when few children had a watch, to get home for lunch.

The noon hour whistle was something that almost everyone identified with. 'Tis funny how the whistle at the laundry was always later if you were near the sawmill, but if you were at the laundry it seemed to be the other way around.

A couple of the men finished their sandwiches quickly, and then got their fishing poles to go throw a line in the deep pool below the bridge to the island. Too soon the one o'clock whistle blew and it was back to work for another long tedious four hours.

Opening Pop and Beer bottles

Every home had a bottle opener or two. Just don't shake the pop before it was opened. There was one amazing and scary person in the neighbourhood who would open a beer bottle with his teeth. However, he expected someone else to supply the un-opened bottle, and it was his to drink if he opened it.

Many Eau Claire boys would pry the cork from the inside of the cap just in case there was a secret prize listed underneath.

Organized Hockey

One fall day the newspapers carried articles about a new hockey association. The Buffalo Athletic Association was to be sponsored by the Calgary Brewing and Malting Company. There were to be different teams and leagues according to a boy's age.

The first practise for all interested boys was held at Victoria Arena. It seemed that in the Pee-Wee division, for beginners, that every boy in Calgary was trying out. We were divided into groups and various skating and stick drills were held.

I was cut, as were many other boys. At least I could see that I needed a great deal of skating, passing and shooting practise. I had a purpose now to learn to play, and I managed, through the winter to improve a lot during the daily shinny games that were played at the McDougall School rink. I learned to sharpen my skates by rubbing them on a pop bottle, and I managed to get a better hockey stick.

The next year I made the Bruins in the Pee-Wee league, and guess what, we won the championship. The brewery had supplied all of the players with hockey uniforms, the likes of which I had never seen before.

The brewery and the Cross family made a positive difference in the lives of many Calgary boys.

Buffalo Association Midget Bronks at the 'old Victoria Arena'

Players include Keith Alexander, Larry Cooper, Mid Houghton, Ron Southern, Billy McLennan, Stevens, Martini, Jury, and manager Dave Duchak and Coach Martini.

The Other Islands

Besides Prince's Island, there were two other islands in the log channel. They were much smaller, but more mysterious. Each of these two islands was covered with a thick growth of willow and brush and their banks were slippery mud, which made it very difficult for small boys to gain a foothold.

The larger of the two islands was called 'The Little Island', as its relationship to the much larger Princes Island. The smaller island, a short distance upstream, went by the name of Beaver Island. Muskrats lived in its banks and ducks nested in its grass. Both islands were the home of many kinds of birds.

Floating in the channel between Prince's Island and these islands was scary because the water was murky, and for all we knew was the home of snakes and monsters. Where are these islands today?

Prince's Island and the Little Island

Our First Home Movie

One evening, after dusk had fallen, several of us Eau Claire boys were walking along Third Avenue when we saw funny lights through the large front window of a house. Being of a nosey nature, we crept up on to the front porch to peer into the room that was the source of these moving lights.

Behold, on a bed sheet hung from the archway were moving pictures of people walking and waving, along a river, with mountains behind. Then there were pictures of bears and mountain sheep. This was wondrous for, we were later to learn, that these movies that had been taken by people other than Hollywood.

Later that year, a movie projector and a screen were set up in our classroom at McDougall School, and the wonder of movies and film was explained to us.

Our Food Supply

Where did the food come from for our family at 711 Eau Claire Avenue? Mom was a good cook and there seemed to be enough food most of the time. True, there were days when she sent me to borrow a little sugar, butter or flour from a neighbour, but this was always paid back. There were times when she would be the lender.

There were several bakeries whose wagons made daily trips down Eau Claire Avenue selling bread, buns and cakes. Two milk companies' horse drawn wagons delivered milk and butter right to your door. The squeaky wheeled wagon of the Chinese market gardener carried a variety of vegetables and fruit.

Adam's Grocery, two blocks away, carried a wide variety of basic goods, and if your credit was good, you could charge for a few days.

Across Louise Bridge was Piggly Wiggly, which later became Safeway. A large Safeway was opened on Fourth Street, across from Knox Church. Here is where we got a lot of bones for McLennan's dog.

There were several grocery stores on Eighth Avenue, but the biggest and best grocery departments were in Eaton's and the Hudson's Bay stores. Here was to be found great varieties of groceries, fruit and vegetables, bakery and dairy products and the largest meat market in Calgary. Sometimes, if Mom had enough money to buy a big order at Eaton's I would take my wagon to haul the groceries home in.

Sometimes, Mom would take me to the creamery on Third Avenue where I could get our enamel pitcher full of skim milk, for two cents. McGavin's Bakery, across Louise Bridge, sold day old bread for five cents a loaf.

Our chickens, in the coop behind the garage, gave us several eggs a day. However, if my father brought home many dozen eggs from the country, we would preserve them in a large crock filled with a chemical substance called water glass. If my father brought home a case full of eggs, he would send me out to sell them in the rooming houses along Fourth Avenue.

Our garden gave us greens in the summer. In the fall, potatoes were gathered and stored in the cellar. Carrots were stored in a box of sand where they shrivelled but were still edible. The back alley was a natural garden for pigweed, which was just as good as spinach. When the puffed wheat factory opened across the road, a pillowcase full of this confection could be bought for a quarter.

Mom was always after me to eat more because she felt that I was so skinny. Thank goodness for that trait.

Our Sarcee Friends

There were times when our Sarcee friends would come to visit. They would pile on a hay wagon, cross the Weaselhead Bridge, across the prairie, through the city and down to 711. They brought food with them, sometimes vegetables for us, and Mom would make tea for them. The horses would be tied to the front fence and we would carry out buckets of water for them to drink. One Brave would stay with the wagon but the others would walk uptown to see and shop.

One day I was feeding some hay to one of the horses. I got careless and besides the hay, my lower arm was pulled into the horse's mouth. It came out coated in green and my face was red after being so sloppy.

In early December the wagon would arrive at our house with a load of Christmas trees. We got to pick our choice and then the Indians would go door to door in the Eau Claire to sell them.

A Paper Route

"Billy, want to split a paper route?" It was my friend Derek; his older brother was dropping his Herald route, which covered several blocks of Second and Third Avenues, as well as some of the houses on the side streets.

"Just wait, I will ask my Mom if she thinks it's a good idea." Mom was reluctant to agree as her opinion of my responsibility was not the best, and she reeled off a list of the problems I could face.

Anyway, Derek and I hopped, skipped, ran and walked to the Herald, found the circulation manager and made application for his brother's route, which was reluctantly approved.

We purchased his brother's old rag-tag Herald bag from him. When I put the bag over my shoulder, it dragged practically on the ground. However, Mr. Summerville, the shoemaker, shortened the strap for a quarter.

His brother now wanted to sell us his list of customers, but his mother and her broom quickly changed that. This route would be a cinch and money would be easily earned each day. However, little did we realize how heavy forty odd papers were each afternoon, six days a week. However, we soon put the old wagon, with a bent nail to hold the wheel on, into service. Then there was the extra time to collect 25 cents each Saturday afternoon; people not home, people without money, customers who claimed that they had already paid, deductions to be made for ripped or supposedly incomplete papers.

The first day that the rain hit in the middle of the route, meant delivered wet papers and a nickel off to several customers on collection day. My dad found me a piece of canvas to help keep the papers dry.

That route lasted till September and we were back in school, but later there were other routes, both Herald and Albertan, not to mention flyers.

Papers from Scotland

Several times a year my father received a packet of newspapers from his parents in Scotland. The mystery of how mail, with strange postage stamps, was able to be transported across an ocean and then across Canada was magic in itself.

In those days, we received two mail deliveries a day. Addressed envelopes were the basis of mail, and there was little, if any advertising. There was no such thing as postal codes, and letters were cancelled with the name of the village, town or city from which they were posted, as well as the postmark date.

I always looked forward to the Scottish comics, with Rufus the Bear and Roman soldiers in Britain.

Parachutes

I broke Mom's umbrella using it as a parachute during a foolish jump off the garage roof. It was a quick decent, a painful tumble and an umbrella bent and broken.

We made many cloth parachutes using Father's hankies, tied down at each corner by string and the four strings attached to a large bolt.

The chute was rolled up and thrown as high as possible. With a good throw, and luck, the chute would untangle itself and float gracefully to the ground. We experimented using larger pieces of cloth, shorter or longer strings, and various weights. Sometimes, several of us boys would hold a competition from the top of the fire escape at McDougall School. Whomever's parachute drifted the furthest was the winner.

One time we took our parachutes up to the roof of the Herald building. One person would wait on the street to retrieve them. Unfortunately, one descending chute landed on a ladies hat and her yell brought a policeman around quickly.

Parades

Parades were a great part of the children of Eau Claire's lives, for it was not much more than a hop, skip and a jump to the parade routes.

Stampede Parade, the Christmas Parade, Salvation Army, Church parades and the army and navy, who often marched from the Armoury or the naval barracks located on Seventh Avenue.

The sound of a marching band coming from the south acted as a Pied Piper, luring children to the parade route, even if mothers had forbidden them to leave the yard.

My youngest memories of the Stampede Parade were not of horses, part of our lifestyle, but of the immense vegetable and fruit costumes worn by those invisible people inside. However, how is a young child to know this?

When I was seven, and my brother five, we rode in the Stampede Parade, I as a cowboy on Teddy, our Shetland pony, and my brother, Bobby, as an Indian on a borrowed pony. I had on my cowboy outfit, including boots, chaps, vest, straw hat, kerchief and gauntlets, otherwise known as gloves. Mom made Bobby an Indian costume out of gunny sacking, and our own chickens provided the feathers for a headband. Bobby wore the beaded moccasins that Mrs. Starlight of the Sarcees, an old family friend, had made for me.

Mom led us to the parade start, and then we were on our own. We stayed on our horses for the parade route, and then made our way home.

Paths by the River

There were many paths through the trees and bushes along the Bow River. Across the road from 711, behind Tommy's, there were several short, but wiggly paths that worked their way down to the rocky shores of the river. These paths had been lined with stones and boulders from the river. Besides adding shape, form and colour to the paths they helped to say, "These are our paths."

The main path followed the shore of the river downstream to the mud hole and then east towards the sawmill. However, the bank became steep and the path disappeared.

In the bushy area around the mud hole, there were many paths that went any which way through the willow patches.

Many of the paths had names, but these names might change from one summer to the next. As well, what one boy might call a path, it might go by another name to someone else.

Sometimes we would put up small cardboard signs, attached to a branch, with the trail or paths name on it - Rabbit Way, Chick-a-Dee, River View, Whispering Trees, Hobo Hideout, to name a few. Names of flowers and animals were often used.

Many a game of hide and seek, cowboys and Indians, and war games were played on the paths and in the bushes. If I ran one mile on these paths in the summer, I ran a thousand miles.

Paths in the Trees

Tommy lived across the street. Behind his house, in a small structure, lived blind Mr. Campbell and his wife. The riverbank land behind here was a small forest, mainly poplar trees and brush. It was a quiet area, with only the sound of the river. The woods stayed cool under a covering of leaves and the influence of the river. Here the low, flat, riverbank was heavily covered with rocks and boulders. On some of these rocks, we used crayons to draw patterns on, and then we threw them in the river.

One day we decided that this woodlot, that we called the Magic Forest, should have a path through it to the river. Now there were some paths there, narrow with the scrub scratching your legs and getting in your eyes. We took a small saw and a butcher knife and removed the branches to widen the trail.

Then, with three boys working, we carried rocks from the river and lined the path. The following day, between swims in the river, we cut more paths and lined them with rocks. Some paths headed to the river, others just wound through the trees.

By building the paths, we added to our sense of accomplishment. We invited out mothers down to share this feeling and to enjoy the paths.

Paying the Rent

On a day, about the end of the month, my mother would call me to take the rent money down to the landlord. I considered this to be a compliment as a huge sum of money, twenty two dollars cash, was involved. Mom would put the money in an old envelope and put it deep in my pant pocket.

Mr. Pickering, the landlord, lived on Eau Claire, but in a house east of the field. Mr. Pickering would greet me at the door and invite me in. Here he would count the money, write out a receipt and then take a nickel out of his pocket to reward me for bringing the rent money down.

On the way home many questions crossed my mind - how did Mr. Pickering get 711 Eau Claire; did he have to pay rent on his house, did many people in Eau Claire have to pay rent, what if you could not pay, how many days did my father have to work to make twenty-two dollars? Would I ever be a landlord and have someone pay me rent money?

Pea Pod Boats

Eau Claire Avenue had neither paving nor curbs. After a rain, the water gathered in the hollows on each side of the road. This often brought out small children with small ships and homemade boats.

In late summer, pea pod boats were made and they could sail in the smallest puddle.

With many gardens in the area, we would simply borrow some peas, carefully open the shell, eat the peas, break a matchstick in half and use the piece of wood to hold the shell open. These boats floated well, but they were difficult to sail in a straight line.

Sometimes we would take the pea shell boats down to the Bow where we would race them. Unfortunately the boats all looked alike, so it was difficult to tell who really won - and then the boats floated down to the sawmill.

Peavey Poles

If the Eau Claire boys had someone whose work skills they admired it was that of the lumberjacks and river men working the logs on the river with their peavey poles. Boys, often unknown to their mothers, would be on the logjams on the river attempting to find the key log to unlock the jam.

In order to help keep their balance, and to push and direct logs, the lumberjacks used a peavey, a long pole with a sharp metal tip and a hinged hook a short space back from the tip.

We would find a good, but shorter pole, pound a long nail at an angle through the head. It was not as long, not as efficient, but it was our own peavey pole. If we were not sorting out logs we used the pole to help with balance as we mounted loose flowing logs that were often spinning in the water as we attempted to ride them down the log channel.

Pinheads, Tadpoles, Minnows, Fingerlings, Fryers

Playing at the Bow River was almost a daily occurrence in the lives of Eau Claire boys. Just a minutes run away from 711 was the Mud Hole, a channel which angled from the Bow, drained south, then angled behind the houses on Eau Claire Avenue, east of Fifth Street, to return to the Bow near the sawmill fence. This channel had a deep pool (the mud hole) and grassy channels that were the birthplace and home of several types of fish in various growth stages. The very smallest which were called 'pinheads', so small that their heads appeared to be just that. Tadpoles were the beginning of frogs, but we lumped in baby fish of about the same size; then there were minnows, varying in length from about half an inch to two inches. Larger than that were called 'fingerlings', and those the legal fish catch length went by the name of 'fryers'

Whether these names or this classification was used by anyone but the Eau Claire kids, I do not know.

Mom's sealers were often used to catch the little ones. This was done by tying a strong string around the screw top, laying the bottle in the water, and after some fish had wandered into the jar, gently pulling it out of the water. Sometimes we sold the bigger minnows to fishermen for bait. Sometimes we feed them to the cat. Larger fish, if Mom did not want to cook them, were taken to the shops in Chinatown where we would barter, asking a dime, but more often settling for a nickel.

Pinhole Camera

One old ragtag issue of the Popular Mechanics magazine had an article on how to make a pinhole camera. It looked easy; it sounded easy.

We got shoeboxes, cardboard, pins and paper, but try as we might the project never seemed to work. We took Dad's box camera, without his permission, opened it, tripped the shutter and peered into the windows and holes, but we still did not understand how it worked. We were no better off in finishing our homemade camera. Nor could we afford the price of a role of film.

Pitch-A-Penny

I wish I had a penny for every turn of pitch-a~penny that I have ever played. The easiest game to create; a game of chance, some luck, but mostly skill.

How was it played? Find a paved walk beside a solid wall, mark off your standing line and pitch your pennies against the wall. The owner of the closest penny to the wall wins all the rest.

Throw your coin too hard and it generally bounces away. Roll it and it might just roll out a side boundary. Concentrate and slide it flat so that it just barely touches the wall. Good! Pick up the pennies of the other players.

What if it's a tie? Just divide the other coins, or have a shoot off.

Who goes first - the winner naturally, and then in reverse order of finish the others pitch.

A nickel gave you five pennies, and sometimes this could be an hour of fun. Perhaps you might end up with a nickels worth of pennies.

Playing on the Ice

'Knock, Knock' "Come on Billy, the ice is hard enough to slide on; the river broke through upstream and there is a long, beautiful smooth patch just behind Buddy's house."

I turned and looked at my mother, who was kneading dough for making bread. Without even a glance my way she said, "What has your father told you about being on the ice? You will get it when he gets home."

"Oh Mom, we will just throw some stones across the ice. I will be very careful." I put on my jacket, fastening the buttons crooked, and my tweed hat and my mitts, which were made of old socks. I said to Tommy, "Let's run before she calls me back."

When we got to the river I saw that Tommy was right, for overnight the Bow's water had broken through further upstream and had left a smooth coating overtop of the older, crunchy ice. Ignoring my mother's advice, we ventured onto the new ice, testing its strength. Then, satisfied with its safety, we took 'build up speed runs' along the rocky bank, and then we slid across the new ice, seeing who could go the furthest, and with each slide, working our way downstream.

Then the inexplicable happened. My slide carried me on to wet, slushy ice, which stopped my feet, but my body carried forward and I pitched backwards into about two inches of cold running water. I was soaked from my hat, down my back, my trousers, long johns and into my boots.

Quickly running home, I could feel the clothing on my backside beginning to freeze. I opened the back door and, holding back a tear said, "Sorry Mom, the ice was wet along the edge."

"That river will be the end of you yet; did I not tell you to stay away from the ice. Just wait till your father gets home."

The Police are Here

There were few paved streets in Eau Claire and there were many rocks along the edge of the roads. A bit of teasing and a few harsh words between boys and the rocks would begin to fly. If someone stood near a puddle then a rock was thrown so that it would splash them. Throw another to scare them, but be careful because you might get two back.

One day during a verbal battle, probably over nothing, with Eugene and his brother, someone misjudged his aim and a rock went through the front window of the corner house on Second Avenue.

The owner came out and naturally, none of us had thrown it, each blaming the other side.

The next day the Black Maria arrived at my house. In it, besides a policeman, was Eugene and his brother. The policeman invited me in. He drove back to Second and stopped in front of the house where we had had our rock fight. We got out and were marched over to the front window, which was not completely shattered, but had a hole in it.

None of us would admit to the damage because we did not know whose crooked aim had been responsible. The officer pointed out that we were all to blame and as such had to share the dollar cost to have the glass replaced.

My parents were rather distressed and ordered me to stay away from those boys on Second Avenue.

The Potato Patch

"Mom, I am going to play in the jungle," Billy said to his Mom, as she stood on the back porch shaking the dust mop.

"Fine, but be careful where you are walking, and do not break any of the plants. Let me know if you see any potato bugs."

Potato bugs, that is a clue as to where the jungle was. Yes, the jungle was the potato patch in the garden beside the house. The spud patch was twenty rows long, each row with about twelve plants.

Billy had helped his dad plant the potatoes in May. His Dad dug the hole and Billy dropped a piece of cut potato with an eye in it into each hole, attempting to keep the potato eyes up to help it sprout in the right direction. As the potatoes grew in the summer, Billy liked to use the garden hose to spray the potato patch. He also used the hoe to pile the dirt up around the plants and to get rid of the weeds.

To Billy, the mature potato plants, when looked through from close to the ground, were like a jungle found in far off Africa. Dirt could be banked to form little ponds filled in with the garden hose. The jungle was now ready to be explored and developed.

Billy would put his lead toy soldiers along with the miniature farm animals on the boat he had made out of a piece of tapered wood with thread spools on the deck. Matchboxes, with doors and windows cut in, worked well as houses. Now all that was needed was a good imagination and agility among the potato plants.

The Princes' Island Stream

In the middle of Princess Island was a small stream that had its beginnings from a spring, and then it meandered through the bushes to finally empty in the channel downstream from the sawmill bridge.

In the summer, the stream served as a refuge; for it was pleasant just to sit on its bank and watch the water spiders shoot to and fro on its surface.

In the winter when it was clear of snow the creek served as a place to improve skating skills as we swerved around the branches that were frozen in the ice and then rounding the many corners of this little stream that was no more than a few feet wide.

This, like many small creeks or streams that flowed fully or intermittently in Calgary, were altered or filled in the name of progress.

Puffed Wheat

"Billy," called my mom, "come in here, I have an errand for you to run. Take this pillowcase and this quarter. Go to the puffed wheat factory and make certain that they fill the bag. Don't loose the quarter and don't spill any puffed wheat."

The puffed wheat factory was just across the road on Sixth Street where the casket factory used to be. In one corner of the large room was a large tank with wires and pipes and flames underneath. I think they heated the wheat which then by some magic expanded into puffed wheat.

"Hi Billy, a bag of puffed wheat for you?"

"Yes, Mr. Dobson, and Mom says to fill the bag full.

Here is the quarter." He filled the bag from a spout and then tied it closed with some string.

"How many kernels are in the bag Billy?"

"Oh, a million I guess," as I jumped to the ground and ran home.

Purple Toes and Fingers

An Eau Claire boy's social life took place around the Bow River. Mud holes, deep pools, rapids and shallow rocky pools where you would just lie in the water during the heat of the day. We used the river from about the first warm day in May to late into September.

Was the water cold? Yes, the first time you got in. This was accomplished by gingerly walking in until it was up to your waist, rubbing water on your stomach, arms and shoulders, then a quick dunk, then immersion.

After a soak and a dog paddle it was out to lie on the rocks and then back in for a swim. On many hot days this pattern went on from morning to night, only interrupted for a dash home for a jam sandwich and some baby carrots out of the garden. Yes, we drank river water, but only where it was flowing swiftly.

Back to the purple lips, toes and fingers - the extended stays in the cold river water probably altered the physiological patterns of our bodies. I enjoyed the immersion in cold water and still do so.

Quarantine

As I walked home from school, I saw the white sign with black lettering attached to the front door of the house on the corner. Immediately I crossed the street, curious to know the disease, but too afraid to be near the house.

When I arrived home my mother told me that the little boy who lived in the corner house had measles and that the whole household was quarantined. She assured me that I probably would not catch it, but suggested that I stay away from the house anyway.

There were diseases, such as scarlet fever, diphtheria, measles, mumps, polio and chicken pox, and that the City Health Department put up the signs to warn others of the disease.

My mother attempted to explain to me about the germs that caused the disease, but it was all so confusing.

There were some years when there were cases of polio. The radio stations and the newspaper suggested that children should stay away from theatres, swimming areas and playgrounds.

Rabbits

There were lots of rabbits, both wild and tame, in the Eau Claire district. Many of the so-called wild ones had been domestic, but had just wandered away, gained their freedom, and then lived a life bordering on the perimeter of domestication.

There were some adults who kept their extra fine rabbits, often angora, in special pens housed in a garage or backyard shed.

Some fathers helped their children build a pen or enclosure out of a piece of chicken wire. There always seemed to be lots of this wire around; just walk down the back alley and you could find some.

Now most houses had a garden, and rabbits, of course, were right at home in the lettuce patch. This brought about resentment and anger directed towards boys who let their rabbits loose next door to a gardener's yard.

Rabbits were good friends when you were lonely; you could pet them, feed them, talk to them and share your feelings with them.

One of the wonders of life was to go out to the shed one morning and find a mother and a new brood of darling baby rabbits. How did it happen; where did they come from? Once we built a rabbit labyrinth, digging interconnecting passageways of tunnels and trenches covered over with boards, tin or cardboard.

Sometimes we forgot about the rabbits, left their cage door open, and they would get out and into Mom's vegetable garden. She would chase them out with her broom, and then I would hear, "Just wait 'till your father gets home."

The Race Car

One day, my father took me to watch the 'soapbox derby'. This competition was for homemade cars. was held on a very steep hill in Mount Royal.

The race winners received trophies, and I was a little envious of their accomplishments and their cars.

Several months later, my father called me into the garage that he had kept locked lately. Inside was a red race car. I was speechless! Granted it was not as professional or as polished as the cars in the races, but it was to be mine.

My father had made the wooden frame, including a seat. The frame fitted over an old wagon. He and his friend, Brask, had fitted a wheel to the handle so that you could pretend that you were in a car. A piece of tin had been curved over the make believe engine and race numbers were painted on the side.

The race car was homemade, very basic, but it was the only one on Eau Claire Avenue and it was mine.

The race car my Dad built

Radio

How magical was the radio of our youth. The McLennan's receiver was a floor model with an on-off switch at the side and a lit up dial in the middle with the numbers from 500 up to 1600. AM only of course.

Calgary had three radio stations; CFCN, owned by the Herald, CFAC, and CJCJ. As boys, we often visited these stations to peer into the broadcasting booths or the small auditoriums where sometimes live music was broadcast.

On cold winter nights, when reception was much better, it was possible to pick up many far away station, such as the CBC from Waterous, Saskatchewan, Edmonton, Lethbridge, Great Falls, Salt Lake and Del Rio, Texas, which had its powerful transmitter on the Mexican side of the border.

Car radios, or ideas about, were only found in the Mechanics Illustrated or Science Illustrated magazines. The Herald and the Albertan listed the radio programs for the three Calgary stations.

The 'old timers', a live group that played Scottish and Western music, always set my father's toes a tapping. There was the mystique of the show "From Lester Square to Old Broadway' that appeared to come right from London.

Programs such as Fiber McGee and Molly, Inner Sanctum Mysteries, the Creaking Door and the Lone Ranger brought families together around the radio.

One momentous Saturday my father took me down to Adam's Radio Parlour, a commercial store on Eighth Avenue. Here was a magnificent radio that had short wave and a record player as part of its operation. Our record player at home was a wind-up machine, but here was one that was powered by electricity. Oh, the wonder of invention! How proud were we of our father to provide us with 'only the best'

Record Players

The basement of 711 was full of boxes of this, that and everything. One day I found an old record player. The records were not flat disks but cylinder shaped. There were several records, but, as I was to find out, the machine could be wound up, but it did not have the working controls to be stopped. I guess that was why it was in the cellar.

In a corner of our crowded living-bedroom, was a large R.C.A. Victrola. 78 speed records could be put on the turntable, wind the motor up, pull the start switch and the room was filled for about two minutes with music.

As my daily adventures often took me to the White Elephant salvage depot, across from the Robin Hood Flour Mills, where there were sometimes records, which had been collected with many other types of goods. One day I found a record of Argentine music - Siboney and Adois. With a little bit of negotiating I paid a nickel for the record.

Back home, with Mom's blessing I played both sides on the Victrola. The mysterious sounds and rhythm proved to be a new dimension to my musical knowledge. I played this record time and time again. Unfortunately, the steel needles would dull quickly, and there just wasn't enough money to buy new needles.

Recycling

Recycling was a way of life for many residents of the Eau Claire area. Old tires, bottles, wire, wooden and cardboard boxes, rags, clothing and lumber were just some of the many materials and goods recycled under the philosophy of waste not - want not. This does not mean that the want part was satisfied, because, for the most part these were lean and hungry people who were doing the recycling, although that word was not yet in vogue.

Recycling often began early in the morning with a general race by two or three of the local children to scour the bushy areas adjacent to the river banks where the previous evening couples or groups had enjoyed a 'tête-a-tête' and a bottle, or more, of beer. Empty beer bottles fetched 20 cents a dozen, or a single bottle could be traded in at the Blue Label Bottling works located on Third Avenue for a bottle of pop that was not up to retail standards,

At the Alberta Printers building, a two story red brick structure located on Sixth Street and First and Second Avenue, the wooden boxes, that the paper came in, were in great demand by many individuals for a variety of uses. Kids used the covers to build clubhouses along a fence; sometimes a rabbit hutch or a shelter for their dog.

During the war when it was very difficult to buy automobile tires, old tires were fished out of the Bow River, then sold to Hovings, located in the Four Hundred block of Eau Claire Avenue, where vulcanizing and re-treading of the old casings took place.

Periodically wagons, pulled by an old horse and driven by the scrap man or the ragman, travelled the area, with pennies, nickels and sometimes dimes being paid for useable salvage.

Re-using Clothing

Mom had a Singer treadle sewing machine. With this, her skills and determination, she repaired and made clothes for the family. Money that my parents earned went first for food and shelter. With a depression around us, there were few items of good used clothing available.

Mom had the ability to take a piece of used clothing, take off the buttons and put them in the button jar, open the clothing along its seams, use her stove heated flat iron to erase the seam marks and then fit the paper patterns to the salvaged cloth. Sometimes the patterns had been made by Mom out of brown wrapping paper.

The pieces would be cut and then sewn by Mom on her old sewing machine. Watching her foot pumping the platform and the wonder of the power being transferred to the needle that stitched the cloth together was magic.

The pieces of cloth would be sewn together to make boys pants, shirts and jackets. Sometimes the buttons did not always match, but if they were for the fly of your pants, it really did not matter.

Mom could take an old sock, attach a thumb, and you had a pair of mitts. Old bed sheets, with holes in the middle were cut up to make dishtowels or curtains. Threadbare towels became washcloths.

Mom patched our long underwear; long johns were a necessary piece of clothing during the cold winters of Eau Claire.

Good pieces of clothing were passed from child to younger child in most families. If there wasn't another sibling to pass the clothing on to, there was always another child next door or down the street.

River Break Up

A time of interest in the spring was that of the river break up. This at Eau Claire did not relate to the main channel of the Bow but to the log run channel.

Sometime in the early spring, a hole would be chopped in the ice and a tall pole inserted. The purpose of this was that when the pole broke free, such was the opening of the river.

Various neighbourhood people would throw a dime in the collection tin, write the date and the time of when they guessed the pole would fall, and if luck would be, collect the two to three dollars for the closest guess. Most people in the neighbourhood understood and basically honesty prevailed. The children were sternly warned not to interfere, and even more so to stay off the ice during the spring break up.

Interest arose as with the swifter water upstream open water appeared. Sometimes there were channels near the pole. However, its movement was the criteria as to the river's opening and an announcement of spring.

River Ice

The Bow River's ice came in many shapes and forms. Sometimes it looked good enough to skate on, but after a few strides, you would hit some shell-ice through which your skates broke and with a jerk to your back, you would be pitched forward to land on your hands and knees.

Another quick way to stop would be to catch your skate in a crack. There was always a scalp tingling scare when you heard a 'swoosh' and the sheet of ice bent, cracked or settled beneath you.

Sometimes there could be layer upon layer of shell-ice. It was possible to break through many layers and find yourself leg deep in water and up to your shoulders in shell-ice. One claustrophobic time it was over my head. Being caught in these ice holes made it very difficult to exit as the ice just kept breaking away until you reached some shelf ice near the shore. Here the thick chunks, following the contour of the river bottom, sloped downwards, and to crawl up this smooth ice to reach the shore was not an easy task.

Almost all of our escapades occurred in or on the log channel on the south side of the river. We were rarely foolish enough to venture out on the north channel of the Bow River, which resembled a scene from the arctic.

River Logs

The summer run of logs down the Bow River to the sawmill added a great deal of excitement and fun to the boys of Eau Claire. If began with the anticipation of the log run, then the excitement as the first logs came floating, twisting and bobbing down the river. We would walk along the bank, playing the role of a junior lumberjack to push and heave those logs that had been crowded up on the river bank, and as the current turned them sideways to catch in a jam of other logs.

Often we would ride astride a log as it made its way down the river. Great care had to be taken that you did not get your legs caught between the two logs. Balance was very important as each log had its own way of spinning, which could quickly put your head underwater and your feet in the air.

After a few days the logs would begin to pile up, creating log jams. We would use our amateur engineering skills to attempt to find a key log, in other words one whose removal would unlock the logjam.

Fun, but very dangerous, was running the logs. When they were floating loose but close together in the calmer water it was a challenge to run across them without loosing footing, or having one spin out from under your feet. This could result in you landing on your back or perhaps a crack on the head.

If the log run was not heavy, we would find some twine and walk up the river towards Louise Bridge. Here we would get two or three logs, tie the twine around them at both ends, and then float on them down the river until we got to the still and deeper waters of the pond.

There were times, when coming down the river on our log raft, we would see our mother, often with a belt in hand, and "Billy, get off those logs right now."

Ma, Pa and me at the logs

The log run and the old bridge at Tenth Street

River Rocks

The study of river rocks was a lesson in science itself. Where did the rocks come from, how many shapes and sizes, why were some white and others brown, how did those fine white strips find their way into rocks?

Rocks were a great part of our activities. One of our personal challenges was to throw a rock across the river. Depending as to where you stood there were shorter distances and there were longer distances. Basically, the rules were, throw without a foot in the water and hit the other bank. Lots of practise helped us to determine what was the best shape and the best weight to throw. If I threw a thousand rocks this way it would be a conservative estimate.

Another contest was to see who could hit a floating log first. Sometimes the log might be sitting in calm water, sometimes as it came through the rapids.

A fun activity, generally in calmer water, was to see how many skips you could make with a flat stone. Instead of overhand, a sidearm throw would be used. Five skips was good, eight great and ten maybe a record. But who could tell the number of skips after the splashes settled.

Where there was a deep pool, we would 'cut the devil's throat. This meant chucking a rock high in the air so that its speed in falling caused it to break only the surface of the water, producing a sharp sound and little waves.

Sometimes we would take our wax crayons down to the river. Larger rocks could be coloured with creative patterns and then thrown in where the water was clear and we could see the colours and patterns.

In the areas of brush that were along the river rocks, we made paths and lined them with river rocks. Other rocks were used to make small dykes encircling pools where we hoped to catch minnows if they ventured in.

Rocks, if they could be knocked from their frozen hold in the winter, were used to break the ice, or if the ice was smooth, we would have our own version of a curling game.

There were several fences in the Eau Claire area that had been built of river rocks cemented together. Some would call these rocks fieldstone.

When the river was high and the currents were strong, you could see and hear the movement of rocks by the power of water.

Rolling Tires

As was often the case, we would roam the alleys, salvaging what we could, and often this was the old tires. These, if they could be vulcanized, could be sold for 10 - 25 cents each at Hovings, a small tire repair shop, located in the east block of Eau Claire Avenue.

We would roll a 'found' tire down the alley to Sixth Street, then north to home. North of Third Avenue there was a small hill to Second Avenue, hence on to First Avenue, where, if the rolling tire made it that far, Sixth Street ended and there were fences to stop the tires momentum.

The tire would be aimed down the middle of Sixth Street. A couple of flat handed pushes and it was off rolling merrily down the street, which was not flatly paved, and if the tire hit a bump, hole or a rock it was liable to careen any which way to bounce off a parked car, a fence or a telephone pole. With careful aiming and lots of luck, the tire would roll the two blocks and come to rest against a fence on First Avenue.

The real dangers have not yet been mentioned; for if a car or truck were to be passing through on Second or First Avenue there could be a real crisis. Fortunately, for the most part traffic was very light.

One day our biggest shock occurred when, after launching an accurate roll, a horse drawn milk wagon crossed Second Avenue. Fortunately, the horse wore blinders and the driver neither heard nor saw the rolling tire, which passed directly behind the wagon. Other than to scare us, this did no damage, and the tire rolled another block to add again another dent to the wire fence.

Rooming Houses

Sixth Street, Second, third and Fourth Avenues had numerous structures that were referred to as tenement or rooming houses. These were two and three floor structures with front, side and rear entrances. Sometimes stairs ran up the outside to the upper levels. One or two room apartments were the general rule. Most units shared a bathroom and some shared kitchens. Butter boxes were often attached to the outside wall beside a window where food could be stored.

There was little luxury here, but for many residents it was a basic roof over their head'. A bed, a chair, a small table and a set of drawers, or a double compartment orange crate, served as storage. If there was not a closet, a curtain might be strung across a corner. Linoleum covered some of the floors and rugs were few and far between.

Lighting was often from a single bulb hanging from the ceiling. The upper rooms were cold in the winter and hot in the summer.

Many of the rooms located on Second Avenue were rented by women or girls who worked at the Alberta or Premier Laundries. Those who lived on Fourth Avenue often had a job downtown.

Several of the houses on 'millionaire's row' on Fourth Avenue became rooming houses. One of these higher rent houses was the Prince house.

Root Cellars

Refrigeration was a luxury that few of the residents of the Eau Claire were able to afford. There were iceboxes of course, but many did have a small root cellar or underground storage box in the yard to keep produce, milk, meat or lemonade cool during the warmer months.

Our cellar consisted of a cylinder box, about two feet in diameter and about three feet below ground, made of wood and with a hinged lid.

Besides being used for food storage, the boys found use of the cellar as a hiding place, or sometimes, unluckily for the hider, as a jail. To be caught inside with the lid down could mean that a friend, or enemy, could fasten the clasp or even sit on the lid. This was a sure way to raise the anxiety and bring about shouting and pounding of the poor soul trapped below, where invariably a black beetle or daddy long legs was in residence.

The Rope Swing

On the South side of Prince's Island, beside the small lagoon separating the two islands was a cottonwood poplar tree with a rope swing. It hung down over a pool of water whose bottom was mud and sticks. The bigger boys used the rope, swinging out over the water and trying to cannonball so that their feet would not get stuck in the mud.

Fear and trepidation preceded the first attempt on the rope. Dares and excuses were frequent. However, after the first swing, if it were successful, we joined the big boys.

Rugby

The boys of Eau Claire played their own version of rugby. The older boys and young men would do a lot of kicking, passing and catching in the field located between the two Eau Claire blocks. We played with an old ball, the sewing at one end frayed and the leather split. We carried this ball with us when we went up to Mewata Stadium to watch the men's rugby games, although they called it football.

Finding a grassy piece of ground that was big enough to do some running on was not easy, but by travelling a little further, we could use the lawns around the courthouse.

Games were of various lengths and various rules borrowed from rugby, rugger and football, probably a combination of all three. We probably spent as much time going over what could or could not be done as we did playing.

One fall Saturday afternoon, good weather, equal teams and with some co-operation with the rules, we were having a great game on the lawn at the front of the courthouse. We scored on a long run and then pinned the ball for a kick-off. Bobby was holding the ball, Bobby was afraid his hand would be kicked, Bobby let go too soon, the ball was crooked when I kicked it, the ball veered sideways and - CRASH! - one of the large lights on the front steps flew to pieces. One of the players grabbed the ball and dashed around the corner and down the street went the players of the two rugby teams.

It was a long time before we played at the courthouse again. Whether we did the right thing by running away is debatable.

A Sailor Suit

One day after school, Mom walked in carrying a large paper bag.

"What's in the bag Mom?"

"I will show you after supper, Billy."

After the warmed up stew and my sisters had washed and dried the dishes, my mother brought the bag out and laid its contents on the kitchen table - a sailor suit, a white sailor suit, blue braiding on the long collar and a sailor's hat!

"Lets try it on, Billy, and we will see what alterations I will have to make." The suit fitted well, but the bell bottomed pants and the jacket's sleeves would have to be shortened.

A few days later, Mom gave me the suit to put on, and it fit just perfect. My sister lifted me on to Teddy, my pony, and around the block we went, displaying my sailor suit to my neighbourhood, which was a long way from the ocean. Sadly, I soon outgrew the sailor suit.

My sailor suit attire

My horse Teddy

Salvaged Tires

During the war, there was a great shortage of tires for automobiles and trucks. Any tires that were manufactured were for military vehicles. Anyone with a car had to look after their tires and tubes. My father's tubes were covered with patches, and he kept a pile of old tubes just in case. In the summer, the tubes came in handy for floating down the river.

Hovings, located further east on Eau Claire Avenue, had machinery to install new tread on tires. Backyards, alleys and trash piles were cleaned up of tires that could be sold at Hovings for up to a dollar each, although most only fetched a quarter. Now, the Eau Claire boys realized that there were many tires in the log channel that had been rolled onto the ice in the winter or rolled over the bank in the summer. We recruited our dads to fish out what we could, made some money, cleaned up the river and helped to keep Calgary's cars running.

Salvation Army Band

Tambourine, cymbals, base drums and coronet, these were the musical instruments that made up the Salvation Army Band. On one or more evenings a week the Citadel Band played on some corner not too far from home. A favourite spot was outside the C.P.R. station, but if it was felt they could sway a potential convert the band would play almost anywhere.

Several ladies would lead the audience in singing. One of the favourite hymns was 'Onward Christian Soldiers'.

There were many down-and-out families in the Eau Claire, but if circumstances became dire, the Salvation Army would lend a helping hand.

Saskatoon Picking

On a day in late summer, we would all pile into Pa's car for a Saskatoon berry picking expedition on the hillside behind our friend Alf's in Bowness.

The only way to get there was across Louise Bridge, out Bowness Road, past Montgomery, where several families lived in cellars, which had no structure above the ground, then over Shouldice Bridge and through Bowness, where there were very few houses.

Hopefully we arrived at Alf's without the frustration of a flat tire. Mom would pass out jam or honey pails to the family and then we would scale the hill to where the best berry bushes were. Mom's pail would be filled long before the bottom of mine would be covered. However who could resist eating two berries for every three that went into the pail.

Mom preserved most of the berries, but for a week, we would have Saskatoons for dessert.

A Saturday Downtown with 37 Cents

With 37 cents in my pocket, earned from selling boxes and bottles, a Saturday of adventure and entertainment was to be had downtown. Downtown or uptown, both terms were used, it just depended upon where you lived. As there was a slight hill from Eau Claire to Fourth Avenue, the 'up' could perhaps apply.

First a stop at the Wave Light Lunch on Eighth and Fifth Street West. This was a good place to read comic books for a few minutes; nobody ever bothered you.

A block to the east, at Fourth Street, the Puss-in-Boots Café and a café housed in an old railroad passenger car, invited one to spend 25 cents for an ice cream soda.

Across to Eaton's, where there was a grocery and meat department in the basement. Here, with luck and the right clerk, two cream cookies could be bought for a penny.

The Heintzman Music Store, only one of two stores on the south side of Eighth in the block east of Third Street, brought a child face to face with grand pianos, musical instruments and 78 play records. What great urges to touch the keys or pluck the strings, but there was always a stern looking clerk to shoo you away.

The delights of the 5 and 10-cent stores, Kresgie's, Woolworth's and Metropolitan were many for any child: toys, books, fishing supplies and gold fish could account for an hour. Each store had its own soda fountain where sodas or sundaes could be purchased for 10 or 15 cents, cheaper than cafes. You could spin around, and around, the high seats as you ate your treat.

Near Second Street was the Picardy Inn, famous for its wonderful pastry. With luck, there were some day old tarts at half price.

Just down the block was the impressive Palace Theatre, while across the avenue was the stately Capital Theatre, both with good Saturday movies, cartoons and serials, but its too nice a day to sit in a theatre, so onward east on Eighth.

Osborne's Books is entered with reverence, for here are many lovely books, but sold for much more than my few coins. But what a pleasure to see books printed in London, Toronto or New York; pictures of castles, camels and ocean liners; 'dream food' for sure. Someday I will have enough money to buy a book each week - I hope.

Next door to Ashdown's Hardware, the main floor stocked with tools and paint. Sometimes I bought a nickels worth of shingle nails for my boats and homemade toys, but no today. Upstairs was a whole floor full of toys. You played with what you could, but the clerks kept a sharp eye if you tended to linger.

Across Centre Street and into the McLean Hardware, which carried hockey sticks, baseballs and bats. My first real, brand new hockey stick, one piece, no lamination, had been bought here one December day for a 25 cent piece received for Christmas. My very first new stick! It shone with respectability. But the next day, two minutes on the back rink at Buffalo Stadium, one hack by giant Jack Steel, and it was broken in two. No amount of shingle nails and black tape could fix it.

Next door to the hardware, the advertisements at the Strand Theatre showed two cartoons, two serials and a western movie - the cost, ten cents for children. The Strand was older and much darker inside than the Capital or the Palace Theatres. There was an aura of mystery and sinisterism about the theatre, so, unless there was a movie that we just had to see, we stayed away. Checking the floor around the ticket booth for any coins that might have been dropped by the patrons was a common practise.

We looked at the men's suits in the window of George McLeod's store in the McDougall Block. We wondered if there was any connection to the name of our school - McDougall?

Across First Street East was the Public Building, that very impressive structure with its huge columns that seemed as grand as those of the Greek temples we had seen in pictures at school. The post office operated a small savings bank. I had opened up a small account that I had built up to 35 cents, but I lost my book and never saw my money again.

Now the most exciting part of the day began, for in this block were Chinese cafes, with their red lanterns and mysterious smells, the Billingsgate Fish Market, displaying creatures foreign to prairie boys, Jaffe's wonderful used book store, a hodge podge of the printed word, more cafes and second hand stores. Calgary's first Safeway store moved into the north side of the block, and this was a wonder to see, so many groceries in the same store. Well, perhaps, Eaton's and the Hudson's Bay grocery departments were as big.

Second Street East; City Hall and the City Hall Bakery with its lovely poppy seed buns selling at two for five cents.

On the west side of the street was the city market place, stall after stall selling all types of food and produce. My friend Cyril's mother's stall was about ten feet wide, and just basically sold butter and cheese. Long hours for a small return, yes indeed.

Back across Second Street to peek in the doors of the beer parlours, both men's and women's, in the Queens and Royal Hotels. The mystique of tables covered with glasses, the odour of beer, people staggering, slurred words, men hanging around the women's entrance. My father had told me that it was separate drinking in Calgary, but if you were in Okotoks or Cochrane, then men and women were allowed in the same beer parlour. Away we went from the door after the waiter, wearing a white apron, shooed us away.

Around the comer to another interesting block, this was 'old Calgary' . Here was a genuine log cabin that at one time had been a bakery, but it now sold shoes and cowboy boots, mostly second hand. We like to try on these boots and wish for the day we could afford such a pair.

The Variety was a relic of a theatre whose Saturday afternoon programs could not match other theatres for new shows. However, their mid week shows offered amateur talent nights. On both sides of the Variety and across the street were many second hand stores usually operated by Jewish men from Eastern Europe. They were generally good-natured, would let us play, with our limited skills, their musical instruments. We could debate and argue with them, with both sides learning something.

One store had many musical instruments - violins, squeezeboxes, cornets and drums; we would play them all until we were told, "that's enough." We would plead that our dad would be coming in to buy an instrument for us; that often bought a little more time to play.

There were tools to check out, foreign coins and watches in the showcase, Japanese fans, top hats, tea boxes from China; every store had something different.

Just to the east was an old house, which held the Chicken Fry Restaurant. It was run by a family of Negroes, who always had a big smile for anyone who walked in their door. We did not have enough money to eat here, but we would walk in just for the lovely cooking smells.

Hungry as we were, it was back to the White Lunch Cafeteria, located beside the Palace Theatre. Here, for fifteen cents, we got a plate of large, hot pancakes and covered them with syrup.

Arriving home for supper we heard the usual from Mom,

"Don't you ever stay home?" and "what did you do, where did you go?"

As usual the reply was, "Nowhere, nothing."

Saturday Night Hockey

On Saturday night, during the hockey season, some of us kids would gather in a small room at the back of Eugene's house where they kept a wooden hockey game. It had a separate hand control for each goalie and a pull handle to activate the wire hockey players. Often the marble used as a puck would stop behind the goal where it could not be touched by a player, so a push with a finger got it back in play.

Eugene had a Montreal Canadians hockey sweater, complete with assorted holes, so you know who represented the Habs. I had gotten last choice so settled for New York Rangers. Most Saturday nights there were only four of us playing, so only four of the National League teams would be used, but I stuck with New York.

This was the big hockey night in Canada because Foster Hewitt would give play-by-play from Maple Leaf Gardens. During the intermissions, we listened to the knowledgeable men on the 'hot stove' discussions. What magic was it to sit in Calgary and listen to a hockey game from so far away.

Eugene was the dunce in the classroom, but at this hockey game, his reflexes were magic. We would hold a round robin with the winner declared when one player had scored five goals. It is not fun to loose 5-0 to Eugene, then 5-2 to his brother, then maybe a close game to the other player.

Semi-finals and again I would have to face Eugene and hope to score at least one goal. Eugene and his brother would generally be in the final with, guess who, winning.

Funny, Eugene was the best at table hockey, but at the rink, he couldn't stand up on skates.

The Sawdust Pile

On Prince's Island, just north of the sawmill, was a tremendous pile, at least in the eyes of a child, of sawdust. It was hauled over from the sawmill in high side wagons pulled by a team of horses. In that era sawdust had limited use. Some of it was used on butcher shop floors to soak up the blood. Businesses that spilled oil might use it on their floors. At one time many Calgary houses were insulated with sawdust or shavings, but there were few houses built during my childhood.

I, like many children in the neighbourhood , was forbidden to go near the sawdust pile because of the many dangers around the sawmill and the river. Never the less I would forget these stern warnings and find myself drawn to the sawdust pile and its pleasures.

First challenge - to climb to its top. This would be accomplished by two steps upward and one back. At times you could be almost up the side, which would then breakaway and down you would go. Then to try a new slope, perhaps not so steep.

The joy of the summit! You could look across the river and maybe, just maybe, see the top of my house. You could scan the riverbank in case a mother or sister had come looking for you.

You could use a board to give you a footing to leap off into space to land in the sawdust below. Or, if not a jump, then closing your eyes tightly to keep out the sawdust, you could roll down the side of the pile. Meanwhile, our dog Sport, frustrated from his attempts to climb the pile, would run around the huge sawdust pile.

Before going home we would very carefully brush all the sawdust from our clothes and out of our shoes. However we would often get caught. Mom had that height ability to peer into my curly hair and pull out some sawdust.

"Billy, I thought I told you to stay away from the sawmill!

The Sawmill

In June of 1856, a group of sawmill men, mainly Norwegians, arrived in Calgary to help develop the Eau Claire sawmill. They lived in tents that they had pitched near the banks of the Bow River at the location of the projected mill.

The mill machinery came from Eau Claire, Wisconsin by way of Winnipeg, where it was reloaded on the C.P.R. rolling stock. Everything for the mill had to be brought to Calgary, as there was very little in supply in this settlement.

The men spent the summer building the mill, then in the fall they worked on driving piles, building platforms and preparing the log channel. After the river froze, they were able to drive piles for the log booms. The first logs, used both for construction and for the mill, were brought to Calgary from Banff on the railroad.

When the river level dropped in the fall, the log channel, which extended to about Eleventh Street, was constructed. The channel was deepened by dredging the gravel from the south bank and the riverbed and piled about a third of the way into the river, creating a long strip island there and a log channel on the south side of the river. Horses pulled a scoop bucket with a handler driver behind the scoop to control the horses and help dump the bucket.

The first log drive on the Bow River took place in the spring of 1887. This proved very difficult due to the rapids, falls, obstacles and windfalls. Six of the log drivers were killed when an unexpected strong current, as a result of a heavy rainstorm, pulled their boat toward the falls. The boat, holding nine men, was steered towards the right side of the falls. The log drivers managed to get through the first two drops, but the boat was flooded during its passage during the third and last falls where six of the men were thrown out of the boat and were killed by the protruding rocks. Five of the bodies were located in logjams during the summer, but the sixth body was never found.

The first log drive was not all that successful, and it took most of the summer for it to reach the mill at Calgary. During the winter of 1887-88, the Eau Claire Company joined forces with a land agent by the name of Marsh to drive piles and the supporting deck for a bridge, named the Bow Marsh Bridge, to cross the river near Tenth Street. Both the town and the North West Territories Assembly contributed towards the cost of the bridge. The bridge went out in a flood several years later.

In 1883, a log dam was built on the north side of the river to capture logs, which were then directed to the south log channel.

Two logging camps had been established, one on the Bow River at Silver City, west of the town of Banff, and the second one on the Kananaskis River.

Each log was stamped on each end with the Eau Claire brand.

Log drives took place each spring, after the ice in the river had broken up. Three to five million board feet of timber was cut and moved to the riverbank each winter. The log drives extended along the rivers for upwards of ten miles and moved about three miles a day. As many a forty men, utilizing peavey poles, followed the drive downstream, breaking up logjams and rolling logs off from the riverbanks.

The logs, spruce, jack pine and some fir, were cut in either 12, 14 or 16 foot lengths; most were eight to sixteen inches in diameter.

When the drive reached Calgary, many of its citizens walked to the river to view the logjams that extended from the millpond, filling up the log run to past Tenth Street.

Later a low area between Fifth and Sixth Streets, north of First Avenue, was deepened to serve as a log pond.

The School Field Day

In early June, the Calgary junior high schools held their athletic day at Mewata Stadium. For those of us at McDougall School it was just a short walk from home to a park where we spent many hours playing soccer on the pitch, running the track and jumping in the pits.

At McDougall, sprint practises were held on the playing field, but training for the distance run was done around three sides of the block using the sidewalk, with little room to pass and two sharp and dangerous corners.

The McLoy System, a combination of age, height and weight, determined as to whether you were junior or senior. Naturally, as the second smallest boy in the school, I was a designated junior.

The week before the athletic day, Mr. McRae named the team members and I had been picked to run the distance race, a run of 300 yards. Now if only my shoelaces did not break.

The stadium was packed with students and teachers from Calgary's junior high schools. McDougall was not one of the larger schools, and we knew that there would be lots of talent from what we considered to be important schools'

One of the teachers used a megaphone to organize the races, beginning with the sprints. McDougall won two of the girls 75 yard dashes and, as well, one of the boys!

Now it was time for the 300 yard or distance races. Mr. Megaphone invited all participants to meet at the starting line at the far corner. Living close to Mewata had given me the opportunity to practise on Mewatas cinder track, and there were many competitors who had never had that opportunity.

The junior boys lined up, and because I had dilly-dallied too long I found myself on the outside end of the line. The gun went off and the other competitors were two yards out before I woke up. However, I knew the track and soon caught up to the back of the pack, then slowly moving up to sixth, fifth, forth, closer to the leaders, then on the final straightaway, with the crowd cheering, crossed the finish line in third place and a ribbon!

I was thankful that the laces of my black high top running shoes had not broken.

Schooling

Prior to the turn of the century, students from the Eau Claire district could have gone to school at the school house located on Ninth Avenue East, and by 1885 in the classrooms above Freeze's store located at 234 - 8 Avenue East. By 1888, some classes were held in the basement of Knox Presbyterian Church, and in 1890 above the jail in the town hall.

In 1887 a four room school, to be known as the Union School and later as Central School, was opened on Scarth (First) Street and Northcote (Fifth) Avenue.

Catholic students could walk or travel by horse and buggy to the Convent School in Mission. By 1888, the first high school students were taught in St. Mary's School.

In 1890, students from wealthier families in Eau Claire could have attended Bishop Pinkham's Parochial School.

In 1892, an addition was made to Central School, which now had electric lights.

By 1903, the City Hall School, otherwise known as Sleepy Hollow School, handled the high school students.

The new sandstone Central School, later to be called James Short, was officially opened in 1905.

In May of 1906, the impressive Normal School, just across Fourth Avenue from the Eau Claire, was opened. Eau Claire students who attended classes here were utilized to train the normal students. In 1922, the Public Board purchased the building, which was to house grades one to eight. By the following year, the new Central Collegiate Institute was ready for high school students.

In 1907, Jewish students from the Eau Claire area could attend the Talmud Torah, which operated in a classroom.

High school and music students could attend Mount Royal College as of 1911.

The Mewata Park Cottage School, that had housed lower grades for a number of years, was closed in 1946.

Scrub

"Knock, Knock, " Buddy was at the back door.

"Hurry up, Billy, there is a scrub game at McDougall."

"You can't leave until you have finished your supper," said my mom. I ate as fast as I could, then I bolted out the door and raced up Sixth Street to McDougall School where the baseball game was to be played.

Scrub, I do not know where the name came from, but as you arrived and touched home plate that was your number and position on the field. The first three to touch were batters, then catcher, then pitcher and so on around the field. Sometimes there could be as many as six fielders, not to mention rover, infielder, outfielder, or even an umpire who did the calling before he replaced the pitcher.

A few of the kids owned baseball gloves; some just wore a winter glove or wrapped a rag around their hand to soften a catch.

Scrub was softball as opposed to baseball or hardball. It was rare to play with a ball that did not have some loose stitching. Bats varied from slim and small to heavier baseball bats that, due to a crack, had been retired from play at Buffalo Stadium.

When a batter or runner was put out, all the players moved up a position. If you were last fielder the chance of getting up to bat before it got too dark to play was slim indeed. However, if you were to catch a fly ball you would change with the batter. On a rare occasion, the batter hit a fly ball that was caught by the person he had just replaced.

If one of the three batters did something that was considered not acceptable by the other players, an extra effort would be made that would allow the other two batters to get on base before the troublemaker could get home, hence he would be out, demoted to last outfielder. As fate would have it, he could be lucky or skilled enough to catch a fly ball and be right back at bat.

We were always very careful in our treatment of the owner of the bat and the ball, for if he or they left in frustration it meant a task of convincing them to stay. But if they did seriously intend to leave, it meant that they would be treated to a round of verbal insults. However, these differences were few and far between.

As was the rarity of good equipment, so were the number of girls who would come to play. We treated them as Tomboys, but in reality we were happy to have them playing alongside us.

On more than one occasion, a foul ball would end up on the streetcar tracks on Fourth Avenue just as streetcar was coming along. An understanding tram driver would stop his car, get out and throw the ball back. Other times, running late or just not seeing the ball lying on the tracks, the driver would travel right past, with the ball now cut, being bounced every which way.

Games often lasted until it was too dark to see the ball properly. Sometimes parents came to watch the game, or to call their children home.

Scrub was a great socializer and in some cases equalizer, for the oldest or biggest of the boys were not always the best batter or fielder.

Self Esteem

The Eau Claire was basically a poor area. We were aware that further south the streets were paved, houses were larger, many people owned a business and many families had an automobile. How did this relate to our self-image; at what level was our self-esteem? For many, self-esteem meant accepting life as it was and being satisfied with what you had. If your parents were satisfied, you would probably be satisfied also.

There were others who strove to get out of Eau Claire. Some people worked at two jobs. Some families encouraged and pushed their children to excel in school and to go beyond grade nine, perhaps even to university.

Some families, as their finances improved, moved south of Fourth Avenue, then perhaps to districts such as Elbow Park or Scarboro.

How did those people who lived in one of the better districts view the residents of Eau Claire? If you were a professional person, you probably had patients or customers there. Did you give them a break in costs or fees; did you extend them credit?

There were racial groups in the Eau Claire. Were they able to handle name-calling or racial taunts any easier?

Perhaps they were able to say things about themselves and feel comfortable doing it. I think that the philosophy of 'the grass is always greener on the other side of the fence, applied to most of those who lived in Eau Claire.

Selling Lemonade at the Laundry

On a hot summer day, I decided to sell lemonade to the ladies that worked in the Alberta Laundry. Although it was hot outside it was like a furnace in the laundry. The wash machines and the tumblers were on the main floor. Upstairs were the ironing rollers and ironing tables for the hand work.

The laundry was always hot, always steamy, always noisy, and always busy. The laundry people worked from eight o'clock until five o'clock, with an hour off for lunch. It was hot and tiresome work, and I knew the ladies were often very thirsty and bathroom breaks were frowned upon by the bosses.

Mom had a box of paper cups and she let me borrow some. She cut up a lemon for me, reminding me that I had to pay her back. We added water, sugar and some ice chips. They were from the small pieces that the iceman allowed the kids to take out of his ice-wagon.

Mom provided me with a clean milk bottle, and in it went the 'lemonade'. 'On to the laundry', where the back door was always open. The workers knew me, and many had a few coins in their dress pocket or purse. My price was two cents a cup, and I was soon sold out.

I went home and added more sugar and water to the pieces of lemon. I gave Mom a dime for the lemon that she had lent me, then back to the laundry where there were many hot and thirsty workers. Now I charged three cents a cup.

When I was finished, I was left with 32 cents. Thank goodness Mom didn't charge me for the cups.

Selling Newspapers

A mark of honour for some Eau Claire boys was the silver badge, purchased for 25 cents from the City of Calgary, which allowed you to sell the daily Herald or Albertan on the Calgary streets.

Now, having permission to sell, and finding that corner or spot to sell from, was another matter. Most of the lucrative corner selling spots were 'owned' by news hawks, some who were elderly gentlemen, who had been at their own locations for years. Many had their regular clientele who would buy from only them.

Well, a millionaire has to start somewhere, and so I started with the purchase of three Heralds at 3 cents each, a total of nine cents. These were purchased from the clerk in the circulation department next to the alley. The next step was to practise and emit that shrill and singing phrase, "Ca-algree Her-ald, read about it here, all the news."

The first sale was fast and easy, and then I was ordered to move along by the irate regular seller near that spot. I soon realized that if a seller was busy in transaction I could act more quickly with a potential buyer who was waiting; a quick sale, but then there were shouts and threats.

Three papers sold, 15 cents! Back to the Herald to buy five more.

Anyway, at the end of the day, tired and dirty, I had sold 17 papers, had one left over, and made 31 cents on sales, plus a nickel tip.

I was soon to find that the competition on the streets was heavy, so I managed to canvas café and restaurant patrons, and beer parlours although there were some very tough waiters who removed you by the scruff of the neck.

With streetcars, sometimes the driver would let you on to sell, providing you got off at the next corner. This would give the driver time to have a quick look at one of your papers. The Herald had the 'Early Edition' and the 'Late Edition'. The Albertan normally had just the early morning edition, but on occasion, had a mid-day paper if it could scoop the Herald on some important news.

Sometimes, there were 'extra editions' in which we kids would travel the residential avenues from the Herald on Seventh Avenue north to home in the Eau Claire. We shouted the news as we raced along the avenues, and people came out of their homes to buy the paper, which might, for these special occasions, have a red headline.

How good it was to arrive at 711 Eau Claire Avenue, all the papers, except one for Dad, sold, and a warm supper waiting.

Selling War Saving Stamps

One day I was asked, by way of the principal's office at McDougall, if I would sell war saving stamps on Saturday at the booth in front of the Legion on Seventh Avenue East.

They would like me to wear my kilt suit for the occasion. I had to clear it with my parents, who liked the idea.

Further, they coached me in some basic fundamentals of dealing with public and keeping close contact with the money.

Early Saturday morning after breakfast, I dressed in my highland toggery. Mom checked my clothing; gave me a bag with an apple and a sandwich in it, and sent me off to my patriotic call.

The legion people helped me to set up the stand. At first I was a little afraid and a bit tongue tied, but after a couple of sales and meeting lots of nice people I learned to invite potential customers over to the booth.

As the avenue became busier so did my sales of war saving stamps. Before I knew it, it was four o'clock; I was thanked and told to, "Go straight home now."

It was a good feeling to have helped the war effort a little.

Selling war saving stamps on Seventh Avenue

Frank McCool, Toronto Maple Leafs

The Eau Claire's Contribution to the National Hockey League

Service Stations

There were two gas stations located in the Eau Claire district, both on Fourth Avenue. The Louise Bridge Auto Service was located close to Louise Bridge and Patton's Garage was on the north-west corner of Sixth Street. A little further south there were a British American and a Texaco located just north and south of Knox Church on Fourth Street. The Deluxe Auto Service was on Eighth Street and Fourth Avenue.

It is possible that some residences had their own backyard tanks that were found in Calgary after the automobile came into use.

It was at the Patton Garage where I did my almost daily work of pumping gas, not into cars, but from the underground storage tank up to the glass cylinder atop the pump.

A strong arm was needed to lever the pump handle back and forth to fill the glass storage container, which was marked by lines ... one gallon up to twenty.

When the gasoline nozzle was placed into the car's gas tank and the lever opened, the gasoline flowed down by gravity and the amount sold was determined by the rings on the glass.

This service station, like most, had below ground pits, not car hoists, where the mechanic could get under the car to perform his work.

Sometimes my mother would give me a whiskey bottle and a nickel to get some coal oil (kerosene) from the station. (We called it 'coilole' and it was years later before I realized what it was.) This was pumped out of a large barrel.

In December, we did what we could at the station in order to receive a free calendar.

At the British American (BA) station on Fourth Street, you could join the Jimmy Allen Club, which earned you a membership card, a pin and periodic literature about aviation.

Setting Pins

A good way to earn money, but involving hard and sometimes dangerous work, was setting pins at the Olympic Bowling Alley, located on Eight Avenue West.

Although you were supposed to be twelve years old to work there, as long as you could handle the work they hired you. Two leagues each evening, three games each. By the end of four hours every muscle in your body ached, and your skin might too if it had been hit by a wayward pin.

Sometimes at the end of their games, the players might slide a quarter or two down the alley to tip you for your good work.

You got home late and your parents were in bed. Thanks to some extra effort by your Mom, you were able to get up and get to school on time.

Sidewalk Lines

The lines between sidewalk blocks were thin and not very deep, but they served many a purpose for the children of Eau Claire.

If you were running, or even walking for that matter, it was bad luck to touch a line, or a crack as we called them. If your stride was too long or too short, you might just touch a crack and bad luck would be with you.

Sidewalk cracks served as a takeoff line for the broad jump, and to get past the next crack was a more than five-foot leap.

Sidewalk cracks served as markers or boundaries for hopscotch, skipping rope and may I.

For very small children the cracks on each side of their house lot marked their limits of play or travel. With older children, the boundary miaht be the sidewalk itself, but not to get off it or cross the road.

When two boys got into an argument and really did not want to fight, the sidewalk crack between them divided their territory, over which words flew but bodies were kept back.

Silver Paper

"Gold is the best, and silver is next. So if we gather silver paper, lots of it, we can sell it for money."

Cigarette boxes - Sweet Caporal, Players - they had silver paper in them, and there were lots of boxes lying around the streets. It was common practise for smokers to just drop them where they were finished with them.

Find the boxes and start a little ball with the silver paper, which was a lining for the cigarettes. Keep adding more to the ball and soon you would have a big ball of silver.

"Don't tell your brother, or he will want to find it too. Let's keep this a secret between ourselves."

"Okay, but who will we sell it too?"

"Maybe the garbage man knows, cause he sells the copper out of wire and steel pipe to the junkyard."

Off we went in different directions, picking up discarded cigarette packages and stripping the silver paper out of them. We then realized that some chocolate bar wrappers had silver paper in them also.

Two days later, we met to compare the size of our silver balls. Mine was about two inches around, but Buddy's was much smaller.

"We are sharing, ain't we?" said Buddy.

"No way, unless you get a bigger ball." I replied.

Anyway, we worked on the balls for about a week, travelling further from home to clean the sidewalks, roadways and alleys of cigarette boxes and chocolate bar wrappers. Gradually, the silver balls grew larger, soon to approach the size of an orange.

Finally, one evening, we approached the garbage man who was behind his garage, burning the insulation off of the old copper wire he had picked up on his rounds. The garbage truck was his and he kept it in his garage.

"Where can we sell this silver?" in unison, we asked the garbage man.

"Sell, sell, you can't sell silver paper, who told you this baloney?" he said.

We looked at each other, and then pointed fingers in the same way.

"You told me," I said to Buddy, who then, with a scowl on his face, came pushed me, and said, "Shut up."

Back and forth, we pushed, then Buddy broke away and threw his silver ball over the fence and we went on to another adventure.

Singing

There were many singers to be found in the Eau Claire neighbourhood. Some mothers sang as they went about their daily chores; deliveryman sang, and whistled as they left their wagon on the way to the house doors; girls sang special songs as they skipped or played with their dolls.

Many boys had their own special songs, some were patriotic, related to the war, and some were from the hit parade, as was played each week over the radio station CJCJ. Some boys liked and sang cowboy songs, some from current movies such as Snow White, while one friend was a devoted Stephen Foster fan who would sing "Way down upon the Swanee River" time after time.

Sometimes when my father had a few friends in and a drink under his belt, he would get out his old accordion and a sing~song would take place.

What were the favourite songs that were sung in the Eau Claire: Row, Row, Row Your Boat, Coming round the mountain, Put your arms around me honey, You are my sunshine, Deep in the heart of Texas, I've got a lovely bunch of coconuts, and the song that twisted around many a person's tongue - Mairsydoats.

Anytime we went to a concert or a movie we were obligated to sing both '0 Canada' at the beginning and 'God Save the King or Queen' at the end of the show.

There was a period of time when 'Land of Hope and Glory' was my favourite song, one to be sung while alone on Princess Island. The song to hate - 'Oh, where have you been Billy boy', sung at school with everyone pushing and poking you.

The Ski Troops

One Friday evening at Cadets, the ski program was announced. It was to begin the following week on the hill north of Riley Park. This is where Eau Claire kids often went sleigh riding. We were issued white canvas parkas, mine of which I wore to school all week, perhaps thinking that I might impress someone.

On Saturday morning, we met at the hill where skis and poles were handed out. The boot toe slipped under a strap, and the heel fitted into a spring trap, that held the boot tight but allowed the heel to be raised from the ski.

After a verbal lesson, we started out angling sideways across the hill, reverse and then back across, gradually gaining height. When we finally stopped near the crest of the hill the bottom looked three times as far away as when we had looked up.

The first decent brought falls and fright. However, after a few runs the skill of most of the cadets increased to a good level of satisfaction. I even managed to stay on my feet from the top to the bottom.

The Sky

My parents and big sisters were knowledgeable and enthusiastic about viewing the sky. Eau Claire's lights were few, and if you were near the river, there was little if any light, so it was much easier to view the sky.

The mystery of the moon changing shape and moving across the sky; how often we talked to the 'man in the moon'. There were times we were told to be home when 'the moon came up'

My sisters explained to me about the shapes and figures in the stars. The Big Dipper, the Little Dipper and the Milky Way were easy to see, but the shapes of animals and mysterious figures were not so easy to figure out. On many cold winter nights, we could sometimes see the Northern Lights in all their glory, but to understand how this happened was beyond my comprehension, but what magic!

Slapstick

For many of the Eau Claire boys our ideals included: Laurel and Hardy, Charlie Chaplin, The Marx Brothers and Abbott and Costello. The basis of these actors programs was slapstick comedy; naturally, this silliness became part of our behaviour pattern. Did this please parents, teachers, neighbours or storekeepers - no it did not, but it did allow us to express our feelings in a manner that we could identify with.

Tripping, pushing, imitation, twisting of words and phrases brought about laughing and giggling to ourselves, but too often frustration and sometimes anger to others.

Too often one of us would be removed from the classroom or ejected from a store as a result of our disruptive behaves.

To be reprimanded often just brought about more giggling or illogical comments. How often did we hear, "Get rid of that silly grin.

As we matured we were able to view the same bothersome behaviour in those boys who were younger, and what was right now, seems to be wrong.

Sliding On The Ice

Came winter with the rain, sleet and snow, which after a thaw and freeze provided ice in the hollows of the school yard. Boys and girls would polish this to perfection as they took a long run and then slid down the ice, sometimes staying upright, sometimes twisting and falling.

Who could go the furthest; who could slide most gracefully?

Sometimes there would be a multitude of children lining up to slide. Pushing in line occurred; arguments took place as to whose slide was the furthest. Quick fun, easy fun, great until the school bell rang.

Small Houses

There were some regal large one family homes in the Eau Claire. There were also some very large houses that contained three room suites in which families lived, while others were rooming houses where the occupants might share kitchen, laundry and bathroom facilities.

There were also some houses in the district that were so small that you would wonder how the families that lived there could 'even turn around'. However, that they had a roof over their heads was the most important thing. Small attics were put to use as sleeping space and entry was often by a ladder. Often these very small houses had a lean-to room attached to the back, and sometimes a lean-to onto the lean-to.

Thank goodness for Winnipeg couches that could double as a bed and a sofa. These could be found in any room that had the space. More than one child slept in its parent's bed because that was the only space.

There were families with tents behind the house, and for six months or more, they provided additional sleeping space.

Snow Diamonds

"Mom, Mom, come and see the snow, it's full of diamonds." I had just viewed new, powdery snow, and with the rays of the morning sun shining on it, it appeared that there were a thousand or more diamonds shining on the snow just in the backyard alone.

Mom looked out the back door at the new snow and said, 'Yes, Billy, those are snow diamonds, but they are too small to pick up, so just let your eyes enjoy them."

"How did they get there, did they fall from the sky?" I asked.

"No Billy, they are spread by the snow elves, who only come out of tiny holes in the ground when we get a snow fall from heaven. The snow elves are so happy that they put some of the very tiny diamonds on the palm of their hand and then blow them all over the snow. Snow diamonds are like butterflies, just enjoy them, but do not try to catch them."

"Have you ever seen a Snow Elf, Mom?"

"No, Billy, they do not come out if there are people around, but sometimes if it is snowing late at night you can hear them singing."

"Now go and finish the rest of the sidewalks."

Sock Mittens - Depression Mitts

My mother, as did many mothers on the Canadian prairies during the depression, made mitts out of old woollen socks.

The sock was cut just below the hole that had been worn in the heel. A thumb was made from the material that was cut off, and it was attached around a thumbhole that had been cut in the sock. The better the sewer, the better the mitt. Sometimes extra pieces of material or fur were sewn around the fingertips or the back of the mitt for extra warmth.

One problem of this kind of mitt was that it felt like there were two for the left hand or two for the right if the thumb attachment was not quite right.

Sorting Buttons

It was a cold and frosty evening. The rink was covered with snow, and it was a good time to be inside, but what to do?

"Mom, I need something to do." She took me by my shoulder to the kitchen table and then spread the contents of her button jar onto the oilcloth.

"Sort them out. If you can find sets put them on a safety pin."

Buttons, hundreds of buttons of all shapes, colours and sizes. Would I be able to find any that matched, let alone four or five?

First, I put them in three piles according to size, then smaller piles according to shape and colour. Finding two alike was not too difficult, but finding three much harder. To find four that were similar, that was an accomplishment. Finally, as my eyes grew tired, I had found four small pearl coloured buttons as well as four red buttons, larger and probably off of a ladies coat.

Instead of threading them on a safety pin, I put all the buttons, maybe a thousand, back in the bottle to sort them out again on another cold and frosty evening.

Sounds

The banging of logs against logs in the river, the whine and screech as log jams were created or torn apart, all as an overture to the sound of the movement of the water flowing down the Eau Claire log channel in the Bow River.

"Find the key log, find the key log, " could be heard as drivers worked their peavey poles to clear a jam. Sometimes there was that voice of shock as a lumberman lost his footing and fell into the cold water.

Further to the east, the cutting saw at the sawmill produced an angry and dangerous sound. Sometimes you could hear the slap of lumber against lumber as the yard workers added to the lumber piles.

The colder the weather, the louder was the sound of the streetcars on Fourth Avenue. In bitter weather, the sound could be heard from the tracks on Eighth Avenue or across the Louise Bridge. The clang of the streetcar bell, signalling that the driver was ready to move, also carried to Eau Claire Avenue.

Further south, the railroad tracks provided a clippity sound as freight car and passenger trains crossed over the joins in the tracks. The powerful noise of the steam engines and the intermittent beeps of the steam whistles, the screech of a wheel with a bad bearing and the sliding of boxcar doors restrained by too much rust, all of these sounds were part of the railroad.

The rustling of the river, especially during the high water of late spring and summer was a tranquil sound to help put you to sleep. To wake you up was the cracking of ice during the spring break.

On a Saturday or Sunday afternoon, one could hear the roar of the crowd at Buffalo Stadium as another home run went over the fence. During the winter, the slap of the puck against the boards of the three hockey rinks or the music of the records played for skating filled the air till nine o'clock.

The clip~clop sounds of the horse's feet and their 'neighing' as the milkman, bread man, iceman and the Chinese produce peddlers made their daily or weekly rounds.

The squeak of the doors or lids on the wagons, the clink of milk bottles, the knock on the door and the shout of the bread man announcing, "McGavin's, " or "Four Ex. " The squeak of the wheels of the wagon of the Chinese produce seller, or his voice as he called out, "Fresh tomatoes, good cucumber, nice bananas."

On Mondays, one would hear the soft whine of the clotheslines as freshly washed clothing was hung out to dry and later in the day, if the wind was right, to be pulled in and the clothing taken off the line. On other days, there was the whop, whop sounds as rugs were hung out to have the dust beat out of them.

Sometimes on a summer evening, one could hear the bray of a neighbours bagpipes or the Celtic music made by my father's accordion. There were times when a group of children would gather together to play, in discord, their mouth organs.

Perhaps the sweetest sound was that of those spring days when the robins and other songbirds again returned to the trees along the Bow River. What we did not often hear were the call of ducks or geese that were rarely seen in the Eau Claire area.

Stilts

After watching a man in the Stampede Parade, who walked down Seventh Avenue on his stilts, I felt that I could do that also. How nice it would be to walk down the sidewalk with your mother and be taller than her.

I got some 2 by 4's from the woodpile behind the back fence. However, I realized that I would not be able to hold onto them and they were just too heavy. It took a few days before I found some 2 by 2's that were just the right length in the alley beyond Third Avenue. Great!

Attaching the platforms to them was not easy. After a few bent nails and one split platform, I was beginning to think that the time and effort was not worth it, and perhaps, did I want to?

My dad saw the results of my work and probably my frustration.

"Billy, weed the potato rows and I will make you a pair of stilts on Saturday."

Saturday, after my peanut butter and jam sandwich, I went out the back door and there were the stilts put together by my father. He had attached the platforms and rounded off the tops so that I could now get a better grip.

Getting up on the stilts was not so easy. My father gave me physical support and encouragement, but all I could manage was three steps before I tumbled off.

My friends all wanted to try the stilts, but most of them did not do any better. Finally, Buddy got his turn, and across the yard he went before falling in a heap.

I practised all summer, but I don't think that the circus would hire me. The stilts finally ended up in a bonfire.

Street Games

Many a summer evening was spent involved in games stemming, it seemed, from antiquity, generally taught by the elder children to the younger, with little thought as to where the games originated.

Hopscotch and skipping were two activities, not limited to the girls, but it was they who generally enjoyed superiority in the skills involved. 'May I' in which the contestant was to move along the sidewalk by means of a command to do some bizarre movement. For example, "Tommy, take three giant sideways steps". However if Tommy did this without first saying, "May I" the potential move was cancelled. How often the participants forgot to ask, or squabbles developed as the other competitors disagreed as to whether the movement was properly executed.

Red Light! - another game with the leader hiding his or her eyes as the competitors attempted to cross a distance to the safe line without being seen in movement. However if "red light" was called and a competitor was caught moving, then it was back to the start. It was a good activity to practise honesty and fairness, never though without argument as to whether the participant was moving or not.

Hide and Go Seek - a perpetual favourite, with children hiding behind fences, hedges, cars, clotheslines and sometimes their own mother who had come out to watch.

Stealth and quietness were two necessary attributes of good play on the part of competitors. How often deviousness played a part as shouts rang out, "Bobby, I see you." Bobby, whose hiding position was actually unknown, stands up, and of course is spotted. The finder had to keep a wary eye on 'home' as those in hiding were stalked, as anyone who made it home before the finder was 'safe'

Can-can, a neighbourhood game that had evolved from cricket, which saw juice cans being used as wickets and a baseball bat or a stick replacing a cricket bat. A baseball was bowled down the pathway and the batter attempted to knock it any-which-way, hopefully over a fence. You stayed at bat until you were put out or someone caught a fly, then you would change places.

A Sunday on the Reserve

My father had many Sarcee friends on the reserve; and about one Sunday a month in the good weather he would drive us out to visit them. Probably some of the Sarcees spent as much time at 711 Eau Claire because they would leave their wagon and horses with us if they were going to visit downtown Calgary.

We had to tie the dog up before we left because he would run after the car. If we took him with us to the reserve, there were just too many dogs that he would fight with.

Dad would drive through the train subway, up Seventeenth Avenue, take the Sarcee trail through the army camp, across the wooden Weasel Head Bridge and then take the trail up the south side of the valley. There were always Indians walking the trail, and more than once we would have four or five braves standing on the running boards. If we had a blow out in one of the many patched tubes, Dad would not let them back on the car.

There were several villages on the reserve and Dad would visit families in each. There were always Indian children to play with and we were often active in 'stampede' either riding the calves or roping them.

One day Dad took me into Chief Starlight's house. Mrs. Starlight presented me with a pair of embroidered moccasins complete with the wonderful smell of tanned hide.

The first wedding that I ever attended was on the Sarcee Reserve. There was lots of native singing and dancing. I sat down with my native friends at the wedding dinner, which started out with an orange and tomato soup.

My days on the Sarcee Reserve were some of the best, fun days of my childhood.

Sunstroke

"Billy, get your hat on; do you want to get sunstroke?"

Hats were hot; they fell off; they got caught on bushes and hats tended to get lost. I was always careful with my Scottish tam, but the straw hat I wore in the summer when the sun was hot was difficult to keep on my head. One good thing about a straw hat was that you could dip it in the river or under the garden hose.

Sunstroke was a mysterious ailment to little boys. Did it make you mad and froth at the mouth? Did it put a hole in your brain, and you would fall asleep and never wake up?

Mom was often mentioning sunstroke, but if you tried to pin her down you would hear, "Now, don't sass me young man." I guess the best thing to do was to keep my hat on when the sun shone warmly.

Taking Sport Downtown

"Come on Sport, we are going to Eaton's to get some dog bones." Sport our German Shepherd, wagged his tail; of course he always wagged it when someone called his name.

"Where are you running to now Billy?" called Ma.

"Don't you ever stay home?"

"Sport and I are going to Eaton's meat market to get some dog bones, and I've got a penny for cookies.

"Don't be away too long, and watch out for the street cars."

I attached a rope on Sport's collar and away we ran out the back gate, down the alley, past the puffed wheat factory, through the dairy stables, past Second, Third and over the streetcar tracks on Fourth Avenue.

Then, very carefully, through the Chinese Laundry yard, and a big kick at their metal sign before taking off as fast as our legs could go and on to Fourth Street.

Knox Church looked as stately as ever, and then we stopped to pump up the gas storage container at the Texaco service station. Across the street at the Old Courthouse, now the Institute for the Blind, a Seeing Eye dog was guiding a man wearing dark glasses.

A dash across Seventh Avenue and in the side door of Eaton's, then up the staircase to the furniture department on the Fourth floor. Two reasons for this - I enjoyed looking at the fine furniture, and, the snub of authority by the floorwalker who had, on more than one occasion, told me not to bring my shedding dog near the furniture.

Back down the stairs to the basement, find a box in the grocery department and then over to the end of the long meat counter on the North wall - "Mr. Butcher, do you have any bones today for Sport?"

"Help yourself Billy, but leave some for someone else.

"Don't worry; remember, I have to carry them home."

Teddy, Our Eau Claire Avenue Horse

My father brought Teddy, our Shetland pony, home when I was about six years old. Having grown to this age knowing the tradesman's horses, the dairy horses and our Indian friend's horses, I had already developed a rapport and friendship towards these animals.

I needed a boost or a chair to get up on teddy's back, which then gave you a different view of the world. At first my sister or father led Teddy with me hanging tight to his mane. Falls came often, but you learned quickly to slide the right way and get clear of Teddy's hoofs.

Soon I was able to use the reigns to control Teddy and riding was a daily occurrence. I had some rudimentary cowboy clothing, thanks to my mother's skill with her needle, a straw hat and an old bee-bee gun that did not work, to complete the picture of an Eau Claire cowboy.

If the garden was not in then Teddy could be tied in the yard. Otherwise the alley, vacant lot or anywhere of many places along the river where the grass was plentiful was suitable to tether him.

As I grew, my travels with Teddy began to cover a much wider area. We traveled along the river to Louise Bridge, east to the sawmill, where Teddy would talk to the yard horses, south to Fourth Avenue, but not across, and sometimes dangerously fording the river to the alfalfa patches on Prince's Island.

When I was eight I put on my cowboy clothes, and along with my brother, whose Indian costume was made by my mother out of gunny sacking, rode the entire Stampede route and then found our way home.

That fall I started riding Teddy to school, tethering him to a tree on the Fifth Avenue Boulevard. On the third day Mr. Richardson called me into his office and stated, "You cannot bring your horse to school anymore." And so did shades of the old west end at McDougall School.

Teddy Got Loose

Mom called from the back porch, "Billy, Teddy is loose again and is over on First Avenue. Better catch her fast before she goes into someone's garden."

Teddy, my Shetland pony was tethered over on the field by the playground. If the halter was not tight enough she could pull it over her head.

Out the back gate I went, across the alley and cut through the Joiner's yard, the quickest way to First Avenue. There was Teddy, standing in the comer lot. I pulled some long grass and slowly approached her, calling her name softly. When I was almost within touching distance, Teddy bobbed her head several times, turned her backside to me and trotted across the avenue. Again I repeated the 'I'll catch you process', but again Teddy turned and trotted down the road. This attempted catch, but slip-away process happened several more times. By now I was joined by several friends and neighbours, but Teddy was too frisky.

Just then Mrs. Hansen, who had watched the episode from her porch, came over with a long carrot. "Here Teddy, good girl, have a carrot." Teddy's ears twitched and he turned and looked at the carrot that Mrs. Hansen held out in front of her. As Teddy moved towards the carrot, Mrs. Hansen slipped a cord around her neck. Then she handed me the cord and the carrot, which I used to guide her back to the bridle and the rope where she was pastured.

"Don't forget," yelled Mrs. Hansen, "you owe me a carrot."

A Trip to Waterton Lakes

Although my father took us on many little trips in his old car, the journey to Waterton was the best and most important to me. However, with six of us and the dog in the car travelling for much of the way over gravel and washboard roads, it was not an easy trip. Hopefully, there were not many flats to fix, but my father seemed to take it all in stride.

Mom would pack sandwiches and hard-boiled eggs, bottles of water and some food for the dog.

The journey would take all day, but we would have many stops, either for the tires or to take a rest. The car really did not have much of a trunk, so extra tires, tent, blankets and dishes had to be put at our feet or tied on the roof.

The closer we got to Waterton the higher the mountains rose, with Big Chief rising, it seemed, right out of the prairie. We knew we were there when the imposing Prince of Wales Hotel appeared on the hill.

The campground was located right beside the lake, and there was an outdoor kitchen, backhouses and a water tap.

Some nights the sound of a bear could be heard at the garbage cans, but my father would beat on a cooking pot and hopefully scare the bear away.

At the dock was the biggest boat I had ever seen. How I envied those people who could afford to take the trip down the lake.

I did not need to be entertained and often walked the shore, skipping rocks and riding the logs that washed up by the shore.

One year we stayed in the back shed of Mrs. Platt, Kootenay Brown's daughter. Along her fence, she had attached many strange pieces of driftwood.

If you lay on your back and watched the clouds passing over the mountaintops you got the feeling that the mountains were going to crash down on you. In the eyes of a little boy, the waves in the lake seemed huge, just like the ocean.

A holiday at Waterton was magic in itself.

Twelve Cents to Buy Candy

Wasn't it great to have a little pocket money, to jingle, to rub, to study the King's picture, and best of all to spend. True we kids would try to hold on to our money, to save it up to a dollar, maybe even two. However, the temptation was too great because the confectionary store was full of too many kinds of delicious candy. For a penny, you could buy a treat, but 12 cents worth, that was a rare treat.

"Now keep your fingers off the glass, I just polished the showcase," could be heard. "Don't take too long in choosing; I've got other customers you know."

Yes, I could see that. As often was the case, I was the only customer in the store. If adults only knew how difficult it was to make decisions when there were so many wonderful choices of candy.

12 cents - a nickel chocolate bar, a 5 cents Macintosh toffee bar, a 2 cents bag of pink popcorn with a mysterious prize in it, jaw breakers, bubble gum, fudge, nigger babies, liquorice pipes, cigars or plugs. The jawbreakers were great, but sometimes scary when they got stuck in your throat.

What to buy, a difficult decision. Finally, 12 cents worth was assembled on the counter, then - "Could I change the popcorn for a dark fudge?"

"Okay, but no more changes please."

Off I ran holding the small paper bag of candy, staying clear of the bigger boys who would make a demand ransom if they knew you had just bought candy.

Just down the street I came across a friend, showed him the contents, and then I offered him a choice, but no, he could not put his hand in the bag; I would get it for him.

It was a challenge to make 12 cents worth of candy last the rest of the day; sometimes yes, sometimes no.

Uniforms

Uniforms were part of the way of life for the people of Eau Claire. Mr. Hunter, our resident policeman, could be seen each day walking to work wearing his classic black hat and his navy blue uniform with shiny buttons. Our neighbour, Mr. Theriault, wore his army uniform, including putties wrapped around his ankles. The postman's uniform, to a small child, looked very official.

Milkmen and bread men wore a much softer looking uniforms, but their hats were peaked and stiff, with their city selling permit badge attached to the front. The Chinese vegetable sellers wore skullcaps and clothing without shape or form.

Ushers and ticket takers at the theatres wore uniforms, often with rows of shiny buttons. Their round flat hats were often tilted at an angle. There were elevators in the large stores and commercial blocks. The elevator operators, for the most part, wore a uniform and many wore white gloves.

Waiters wore white shirts and a tie. Waitress's uniforms were normally of a white or pink colour, with the ladies wearing a short apron with the name of the establishment stitched in the material.

Schoolteachers were quite formally dressed, with the men in a long sleeved shirt, tie and jacket. Even Captain Ferguson, who came to the schools to handle physical education classes, wore long pants and a white shirt rolled up to the elbows.

Workers at the Eau Claire sawmill and other manual workers would normally wear bib overalls.

Nurse's uniforms appeared to be heavily starched and stiff. Bank manager's suits were vested and of heavy material. Often a watch chain crossed their vest.

What about the cadet uniforms of the Eau Claire boys? Our uniforms brought us enough pride that we would wear them to school two or three days a week. If you had made one of the hockey teams of the Buffalo Athletic Association, you might wear your sweater every day.

Utopia

For many of the kids who lived in Eau Claire it was the centre of the universe - what else could one need. We had the river, the islands, vacant lots, Buffalo Stadium, a dairy, stores, the grand castle like building known as McDougall School, downtown with its stores and theatres, the mystique of Chinatown, streets, alleys, playgrounds; just about all our 'Tom Sawyer' needs were met.

Perhaps there were some Calgarians who looked upon the area as a ghetto, and perhaps it was, but all it took to move up and out was hard work and a little bit of luck.

This was later shown by those individuals who had succeeded academically and through the professions and business.

Others might have looked upon the district as an enclave, supplying the workers for the sawmill, dairy and laundries. In reality the districts boundaries were blurred.

True the Bow River was the northern boundary, Eleventh Street and the castle like armoury was a natural west side; the east end blurred into Chinatown, but the south boundary began to fade as you passed Fourth Avenue where the roads were now paved, the houses generally larger and the downtown core began to take shape.

The Vacant Field

In the fall of 1939, not long after war was declared, a platoon of sailors, armed with shovels and rakes, marched down from the Naval Barracks, which was located on Seventh Avenue and Third Street West. Their job was to build a parade ground on the open field that at one time had been the log pond.

The area that the sailors worked on was weeded and levelled, and then gravel was spread around.

The parade square was used for over a year, and then plans were in the making by the Calgary Brewing and Malting to construct Buffalo Stadium, a baseball field in the summer and to hold three hockey rinks in the winter.

Crowds of several thousand filled the stadium for baseball games, and when the bleachers were full, the spectators lined the outfield fences. Military and civilian teams competed, and visiting teams included American military teams from U.S.A. and Alaska. A national League All-Star team also played in Buffalo Stadium.

On several occasions, a track was set up and Greyhound dog races were held here.

Vacant Lots

There were many vacant lots in the Eau Claire district. Who owned each of them was generally not known, but most of these pieces of land were generally owned by the city, probably as a result of taxes not paid during the depression.

Many of the lots were covered by scrub brush, and there were many wild rose bushes. Rubble had been dumped in places in some of the lots, and paths had been worn across the space and through the bushes. Some lots, where there was a bit of a hill, had caves dug by boys who lived nearby. Scrap lumber was used to lay a floor or line the walls. Sometimes a hobo would use a cave to escape from the elements.

The McLennan family used the lot on the east side of Sixth Street to tether Teddy, our Shetland pony. No one ever stole him or let him loose, but both children and adult alike liked to pet and feed him.

Some families used vacant lots that were beside their homes for vegetable gardens. However, if they were unfenced there was always a risk of others borrowing peas or carrots, for there were many people and individuals in the district that were living on the 'bare edge

When my father sent me to the confectionary on Third Avenue for a five-cent package of Zig Zag cigarette paper, I would run all the way, both there and back. Part of the route lay through two lots that had a connecting wiggly path that included ups and downs, twists and turns and an exciting challenge for someone who liked to run and jump.

One lot, situated on Second Avenue, between Fifth and Sixth Street, was flooded into a rink by the next-door neighbours whose daughter used it to practise her 'fancy skating' and to play hockey with the neighbourhood boys.

Besides the numerous areas bordering the river, there were at least a dozen vacant lots that were just a hop, skip and a jump from the McLennan's.

The Value of a Dime

Many Eau Claire children had to hustle for a dime - gathering bottles, boxes and salvage, cleaning snow off sidewalks, weeding gardens, selling the Albertan or Herald, hustling the Star Weekly, MacLean's or the Liberty magazine. These were just some of the common ways to earn a dime. A few of the kids worked in their parent's store.

Some of us were lucky to get on at Buffalo Stadium, while others worked at the Crystal Swimming Pool and Ice Rink.

There were occasions when we caught suckerfish under the weir and then sold them in Chinatown, bartering long and hard to raise what we received from five cents to ten cents.

Boxes were sold to Louis Petrie, food wholesaler, who was located on Ninth Avenue and Sixth Street. Even though he owned the company, he still did the buying from us, one cent for cardboard and two cents for wooden boxes. Liquor, apples and oranges came in wooden boxes, while cardboard boxes could be salvaged behind many stores.

Mr. Petrie, who still spoke with a strong Scottish brogue, kept a little jar of pennies, nickels and dimes to pay the kids for the boxes.

The Savage family, who worked out of their garage, located on Sixth Avenue next to Mother Fulham's house and piggery, bought liquor bottles, which they filled with some mysterious liquid, to be sold for what we did not know.

On some hot summer days, a lemonade stand, made from my homemade wagon, with an apple box on it to serve as counter and storage, was put into service on Eighth Avenue, on the corner of Eaton's store. Sales were not great, but then a penny was a penny and ten of them made a dime.

Shovelling snow from sidewalks earned a nickel or a dime, with perhaps one in ten doors knocked on bringing a job. Perhaps the greatest reward came one day when, after finishing a walk, on Second Avenue, and not a particularly long one, and I was rewarded with a dollar!

The lessons of entrepreneurship came at an early age, but I was never able to learn and practise that Scottish trait of saving money.

Vegetation Jewellery

Making decorations from plants was indeed a summer activity. Dandelion stems were often used to make chains, Pick the dandelion close to its roots, snap the head at someone else, create a circle out of the stems and insert the narrower part into the larger end, add another and then another ring, adding more until you had a chain of dandelion stems. How many links could you add until the chain fell apart?

More secure were rose hip beads. However gathering the wild rose hips took longer, and you needed "Mom's", needle and some thread.

Vick's Vapour Rub

In the winter, our house was warmed by the kitchen stove or the living room heater, but upstairs and in the corners, it could be quite chilly. Classrooms at McDougall could be the same way, and it seemed that most of the time you were either too hot or too cold.

Winter brought colds, runny noses and lots of coughing. If your mother found you with these symptoms, she had a cure that was sure to work.

On with your pyjamas, into bed and then the dreaded Vick's Vapour Rub. The smell itself was enough to gag you. Mom rubbed it on your chest and neck, and then hot strips of flannel from an old sheet were placed over the Vick's.

The heat was uncomfortable and the whole result could be scary.

Did it work? I am not sure. However, it was best to say, "Thanks Mom, I feel better now, cough, cough.

A Visit to the Dog Pound

One day I ran into Eugene and his brother. They were on their way to the dog pound and they invited me along. We walked through Chinatown and got a drink from the water hose at the service station on the comer.

As we walked further east along the river there were houses older and more ramshackle than were in the Eau Claire. Then we came to the city pound, a small building and a yard surrounded by a high fence. From in the yard came the yelping and barking of dogs. Eugene hadn't told me, but his plan was to open the gate and let the dogs out.

He walked around to the office door and found it locked, and then coming around back, he opened the gate.

One dog looked out, then another. Then five dogs, one after another, ran out the gate and took off down the street.

When I got home my mother said, "Where have you been Billy, you are always running off some place." I did not tell my mother about this experience.

War Saving Stamps

During the war the students of McDougall, as were in most schools in Canada, encouraged to buy War Saving Stamps to help the government finance the war effort. Adults could purchase Victory Bonds at banks and financial institutions.

The War Saving Stamps cost 25 cents each and were then pasted in a booklet until twenty, or five dollars worth, filled the book up.

Teachers encouraged the students to show their patriotism and purchase stamps. Some schools had competition of sales between the rooms. Now 25 cents may not seem like a lot of money, but there were too many families in the Eau Claire who were just getting by financially.

The Victory Bond sales provided a great deal of entertainment for the boys of Eau Claire who could walk to the stage that had been placed on First Street beside the Hudson's Bay store. Here, besides patriotic speakers, there were singers, musicians and comedians.

War Saving Stamps helped to teach the Eau Claire boys about saving for the future.

Wartime Dance Halls

During the war, there were hundreds, if not several thousand, of army and air force personnel from several countries training in Calgary. Evening transportation from the camps and barracks was easy on Calgary's streetcars.

Calgary had seven downtown movie theatres and many cafes and restaurants.

However, most of the military boys were away from home, lonely and in need of chatter, laughter and sociability. Here is where the small dance halls or dance clubs served a purpose. With a coffee pot, some cookies, a record player, a dance floor and some hostesses, namely Calgary girls and women.

Perhaps some of the Eau Claire boys hung around the downtown a little too much, but then it was only a few minutes from their homes. Early one evening, several of us climbed the stairs to the Avenue Ballroom, located above the Kresgie store. We were in the door, laughing and pretending to dance, as we made our way to the refreshment table.

"Just stop right there. You boys put your hats back on and head out the door." I jumped a foot, looked around, and there was our teacher Miss Barrel.

We left quickly.

The Wash Basin

Many Eau Claire homes had a washbasin on the back porch. It was easier to carry a kettle of water out to this basin to wash in than to use the kitchen sink. A soap dish sat on the porch and a towel, often frayed or with a hole in it, hung from a nail.

"Don't forget to scrub your elbows, Billy."

The Whale

One afternoon my father came home and told us that we were going to see a whale. Now I knew that whales were very big and only lived in the ocean. I had looked it up in the big dictionary, even if it was falling apart, in the living room.

Anyway, after supper we walked up to the railway tracks. Outside a freight car, sitting on one of the sidings, was a sign, "See the whale, adults 10 cents, children 5 cents, families 25 cents. Paw paid and I was first up the stairs to the entrance. Inside was the biggest, longest and smelliest creature that I had ever seen. You could even reach over the railing and touch it.

It was hard to understand how it had been caught, how it was put into the boxcar and what became of it. I still wonder.

White Rabbit

Do kids still play White Rabbit? Did I play this game; yes, more times than I can count. Did all the boys in Eau Claire play White Rabbit? No, because it was an activity that involved a lot of running, silliness and perhaps inconsideration.

What is White Rabbit? It is simply the act of knocking on doors, then running and hiding. If you felt daring when you saw the person open the door, come out and then looked around, you yelled "White Rabbit."

Was it played on our house? Yes, but we had a bell that rang when you turned the handle. Did I ever play it on my sisters or my parents? Yes, many times.

Were we kids ever caught? Yes, there were some fast runners in Eau Claire. If they knew what was happening they might come out the back door quietly and keep out of sight until you came out of your hiding place.

Did anyone call the police? Not that I know of, but we did receive some threats to have the police called, or to be marched to our parents house where we knew that there would be punishment.

May I say to those we teased, "I am sorry, it will not happen again."

Who Will Get to the Beer Bottles First?

The bushy area around the mud hole was a spot often used by couples to 'spoon' . Few young men had cars and with many people in the area living in rooming houses private space was not easy to come by. In the evenings, couples would come down to the river area to drink a beer and socialize. Boys, being boys, would often tease the couples by throwing pebbles in the bushes.

The visitors would add to the economy of the Eau Claire because they would leave the beer bottles behind, and the empties were worth 20 cents a dozen.

With a bedtime deadline, it was not probable to hang around until the couples left. This meant getting up early the next morning, running down to the river and hoping to find the bottles, not broken or thrown in the river. I knew the old saying, 'the early bird gets the worm', but getting out of bed was another matter. Too often, I would look out the bedroom window, as the rising sun was shining through the trees, and see Dee heading down to the bushes. Most often, he would be first there to pick up the spoils of the night before. Sometimes, but not often, I would beat him to the bottles.

Window Magic Art

Winter in Eau Claire was always cold. The furnace in the cellar sent up very little heat to the second floor.

The middle room, where my brother and I slept, did not have a storm window on it. That was okay because it was easier to stick your head out or to listen to the skating music from Buffalo Stadium.

After several cold nights, the frost on the window glass built up to form many wonderful patterns - feather like, grass like, mysterious and befuddling. How did they get there, what were they made of, how did they grow? Were there any two patterns or shapes the same? I don't think so.

When the sun shone on the east-facing window in the morning, you could see colours in the frost, maybe ever so fleeting, maybe ever so faint.

Waking up to see a thick coating of frost and ice was a good reminder to wear your long Johns.

A Winter Night at 711

Winter nights on Eau Claire Avenue would find little boys snuggled under extra patchwork quilts, socks on their feet and a sweater on.

My bedroom was on the second floor and very little heat rose from the coal-fired furnace in the basement or from the nickel-plated stove in the living room.

The bedroom window, always open slightly, was just single glaze and with a cold spell the ice could build up to half-inch thickness. With a long cold spell, the frost would extend to the wall surrounding the window.

With the cold, the dogs would howl to be let inside. Sport, our dog, would curl beside the kitchen stove, underfoot of my mother when she was cooking.

From the alley could be heard the sound of a neighbour cranking his car in an effort to start it. From Fourth Avenue came the metallic sound of a streetcar, the cold enhancing the sound of metal wheels on metal rails.

On some clear nights, there was the magical glow of the Northern Lights, shining bright, ebbing and creating patterns in the sky in the north.

There was the evening fun of dressing warmly and going outside and trying to catch the fluffy snowflakes that were drifting and dancing down through the light of the comer streetlight.

There was the joy of walking home, feet wet and fingers cold, to open the backdoor and be greeted by the smell of newly baked bread and cinnamon buns!

Wondering

"Billy, lets go sit on the logs and wonder.' This was an activity some of us Eau Claire kids enjoyed as there were so many, many things to sit, wonder about, and share each other thoughts, goals and worries.

In the hot days of summer, we would sit on a log, dangling our feet in the water and wonder about the fall and so many things about school or fall sports and games.

One of the log sitters told us that his mother had said that wondering was 'gazing at God's window." That saying, we attempted to understand its meaning, and this brought about all sorts of wondering.

We wondered about far away places, where the river came from and where it went. We wondered as to how the various clouds above us formed or how the fish in the river were able to breath.

We wondered about our futures, about a new baby boy in one member's family, about old grandparents.

We wondered about sports and the players, about school, and yes, about girls. In retrospect, we had it pretty good, to sit by a beautiful river with our friends and have the time to just wonder.

The Eau Claire District

Bounded by Fourth Avenue - sort of, fading off into Chinatown to the east and edged by Louise Bridge on the west side. The Bow River, on the areas' north side, formed a boundary that was more realistic in its definition. This area was originally part of the land grant given to the Hudson's Bay Company. The Dominion Lands office was organized in 1871. In 1879 land was set aside for the support of railway construction.

The future Eau Claire area was, following the land survey, part of sections 21 and 22. Homesteads of these sections north of the Bow River were in the names of Felix McHugh, Edward Baynes and Philip Van Courtland.

The C.P.R. set up their townsite in Section 15, which had been surveyed into avenues and streets. Its northern section line was to become Reinach (Fourth) Avenue. Third Avenue was called Egan and Second Avenue was Abbott. Centre Street was McTavish, Scarlet was First Street and Hamilton was Second. Barclay was the original name for Third and Ross is now Fourth Street. Fourth was a section line and as a result the streets to its west are not parallel with those to the east. All of the names used were executives connected with the railroad.

First Avenue only went by that name. Centre Avenue became Eau Claire Avenue in 1925. Centre A Avenue, a Eau Claire Company creation, which disappeared in the 1950's, was a short block extending west of Fourth Street, with small company houses just on its north side.

By 1890 that land north of First Avenue and west of Fourth Street was owned by the Medicine Hat Land Company. Eau Claire Avenue was laid out in two sections, a block between Fourth and Fifth Streets and a block between the displaced Sixth and Six A Streets. First Avenue ran west from Centre Street, past the Eau Claire sawmills land angled south just west of Seventh Street and ran parallel to the river to the Bow Marsh Bridge. Second and Third Avenues terminated at Eighth Street, while Fourth Avenue continued to Eleventh Street.

First, Second and Third Streets ran from First Avenue to Ninth. Fourth Street began at the river and crossed the railroad tracks on a level crossing. Fifth Street began on First Avenue and continued to Ninth Avenue. After the log pond was closed, Fifth Street was extended north to Centre (Eau Claire) Avenue. Sixth Street was divided between Centre and First Avenues, being located half a block east and Six A half a block west of the true Sixth Street.

Eighth and Ninth Streets were shortened by the angling of First Avenue along the river.

There were some blocks in the Eau Claire that had alleys, and there were some that did not. Sounds confusing, but it all seemed so natural to those that lived there.

Fourth Avenue was Calgary's first upscale area, and it had many fine homes located on it. The avenue had been paved with oiled wooden blocks and from an early date had sidewalks and curbs. Calgary's first water main was laid on Fourth Avenue east to First Street and then south to Eighth Avenue. Street car tracks ran north on Fourth Street and then west on Fourth Avenue to cross Louise Bridge.

The avenues north of Fourth were not paved but were heavily oiled, except Eau Claire which had received random oiling. All streets and avenues had sidewalks, however only Third Avenue and the eastern part of Second had curbing. Third Avenue had boulevard trees and there were a few on First Avenue.

Eau Claire Sawmill

The story of the Eau Claire mill has been written many times, and so this is an attempt to describe those aspects of the mill that relate to the river and the Eau Claire district.

After the company obtained the timber rights on 100 square miles of land adjacent to the Bow, Kananaskis and Spray Rivers land for the location of the mill was obtained. Two logging camps were established, one on the Bow at Silver City and the other on the Kananaskis. In Calgary a log weir was placed adjacent to the mill site.

Upstream from the island a log channel was created and a log weir constructed on its north side and further upstream another weir was placed across the main stream of the Bow.

Machinery for the mill was brought to Calgary and set up in 1886. By this time log drives were taking place on the Bow River, with gangs of up to forty men moving the logs from the mountains to Calgary. Peavey poles were used to move the key logs and open up the log jams.

Logs were from eight to sixteen inches in diameter and were cut in 12, 14 and 16 foot lengths.

Log drives took place on the Bow from 1886 to 1944.

The mill ceased operation the following year. In its top producing year the mill turned out three carloads of lumber daily, and it was the main source of lumber in the Calgary area.

Gradually improvements were made to the log run; timber shored up the south bank near the west bridge; a bridge was constructed to connect the mill to the island, and west of the island another bridge and a water screen connected the gravel bar to the island. Another small bridge crossed the log channel just west of Sixth Street.

An office was constructed in the mill yard. The lumber was stacked to cure and filled the huge yard.

In 1889 the Calgary Water Power Company's plant was opened adjacent to the mill. A new weir was placed across the Bow west of Tenth Street. This helped to raise and regulate the water level to produce a drop of 13 feet. 700 horsepower and 600 kilowatts were obtained during peak operations. In the winter a steam plant, fueled by coal and waste from the sawmill, replaced the water source. The Calgary Water Power Company was purchased by the Calgary Power Company.

Many of the employees of the sawmill made their home in the Eau Claire district. The six houses on Centre A Avenue were constructed by the mill owners

Many Calgarians would visit the Bow to see the arrival of the log run in the spring. The logs were dangerous to play on, but running on them, spinning a log till you fell off and riding a log down the river were great sources of fun and excitement for many a Eau Claire boy.

A log storage pond was dredged in the low area north of First Avenue, between Fifth and Sixth Streets.

Peter Prince

Born in Three Rivers, he came to Calgary to manage the Eau Claire Lumber Company. Besides the mill he supervised the logging crews that cut and floated the logs down the Bow River to the mill. He, himself, took part in the log drives until he was 60 years old.

Peter was responsible for the first water wheel on the Bow River. This equipment supplied Calgary with hydro-electricity through the Calgary Water Power Company. He invented the sheerboom, an important piece of logging equipment. The first public transport bridge in west Calgary was constructed by him in 1887.

His impressive brick residence on Fourth Avenue was one of the first architecturally designed homes in Calgary.

The house now sits in Heritage Park. Calgary's first skyscraper, the Robin Hood Mills, was one of his projects.

Mr. Prince was president of the Calgary Iron Works, a partner in the Prince-Kerr Ranch, and he was a stockholder in many early Calgary companies.

At age 80 he bought and learned to drive a Rambler, the first gas powered car in Calgary.

Many of the older houses and buildings in Calgary were built from lumber from the Eau Claire mill. Prince's Island is enjoyed by countless Calgarians all year round.

The River

With the establishment of the sawmill in 1886 the main island in the river became part of the mill property.

There were two smaller islands in the south channel and upstream was a gravel bar with images of land along it.

This was to be heightened by rocks and gravel dredged up from what was to be the log channel on the south side of the river.

Log pilings were placed along this gravel bar to a point west of the present Louise Bridge, and a log boom ran across the river to the north bank. Later a bridge and weir, located just west of 6A Street, allowed access to the gravel bar and, as well, allowed water to return to the main channel.

On the south side of the log channel pilings were placed and a crude bridge spanned the narrow channel. A log boom, slightly upstream from the mill, directed the floating logs to a conveyor belt that pulled the logs up into the mill. On the downstream side of the saw mill a bridge was built to gain access to the island, later to be known as Prince's Island.

Prince's Island

When the Eau Claire lumber people arrived in Calgary the island was attached to the south shore by a low berm, which had probably started out as a beaver dam, over which the river flowed during the periods of high water. Along the north east side of the island was a gravel and mud flat. Bubbling from a small spring a meandering creek flowed down the middle of the island. Two small islands were found in the south channel.

There were groves of bush and poplar trees, providing homes for the birds and food for the beavers who frequented the lagoon. The lagoon, with its murky bottom, offered a good habitat for the bottom feeder sucker fish.

Along with the construction of the saw mill a wagon bridge and a foot bridge, located further downstream, provided access to the island, where the saw mill's sawdust was stored.

In 1910 William Pearce, who had reserved much of the north shore of the Bow in Calgary as public lands, proposed a Bow River parkway, with the river front road passing through the island. The master plan, designed by Thomas Mawson in 1914, showed a park with formal gardens, a boating lagoon and a museum for the area.

In 1908 the Anglican Young People's Association opened their tennis courts on Prince's Island. The court's surface was shale and the lines were strips of canvas held down with wire hooks. About 1919 the courts became part of the Prince's Island Tennis Club. By 1926 lease problems arose, play in this area came to a halt, and the club amalgamated with others to form the Calgary Tennis Club.

In 1947 the city purchased the island and some surrounding land for the sum of $11,250.00. In 1953 about 23 acres of underbrush was cleared and a basic layout of a football pitch, baseball diamonds and a playground took place. Dykes were constructed to deter flooding.

Eau Claire Grows

With the opening of the Eau Claire saw mill some of the mill employees built houses to the south of the mill lands. Within two years there were over twenty houses plus barns, stables and sheds in the Eau Claire.

In 1891 land to the west of the mill parcel was owned by the Calgary and Medicine Hat Land Company.

In 1902 Ross Avenue (First) had three houses on its north side. One of these was the home of Reverend Herdman. Abbott Avenue (Second) had ten houses on its north side and fourteen dwellings on its south side. Eau Claire employee Barnett Thorpe built his house here. It was later moved to Heritage Park.

Osler Avenue (Third) had two houses on the north side and seven on the opposite side, but three of these were vacant. This area had been, in the past, used for matched horse races.

The Crick Boarding House was operating on Reinach (Fourth) Avenue.

By 1906 fire alarm boxes 25-28 were in or in close proximity to the Eau Claire district. The Laidlaw Grocery was located at 506 Third Avenue. Richard B. Bennett lived at 222 Fourth Avenue.

Utilizing the Henderson's Directory for 1910 we may note that there was not a 'Chinatown' on Centre Street.

There was not a Centre Avenue or Eau Claire Avenue. No buildings were listed west of Fifth Street on First Avenue. East of Fifth Street were the Eau Claire and Bow Lumber, Calgary Water Power and Prince-Kerr Ranche Company. Second Avenue was the location of a boarding house, Rochon Manufacturing Confections and Henry Crossland - shoemaker. Besides the Alberta Steam Laundry, Opsal Brothers - grocery, Langston Groceries, Ben Robson - blacksmith, and George Bugler - groceries Third Avenue was the location of Fred Langston's Blue Label Aerated Water and English Brewed Ginger Beer. This soft drink firm was in business at this location until 1940's.

The prestigious Fourth Avenue, formerly Egan, was the location of the Bramear lodge, Calgary's Women's Hostel, John McAra, the printer, Calgary City Pump House, the Normal School (1908), Central School, and as well, the homes of such notables as Arthur Wheeler, George Lane, James Wood, Peter Prince, Turner-Bone and George King. R.B. Bennett and James Lougheed had lived there and later it was the location of the Army and Navy Veterans of Canada.

The Calgary Cartage Company stables were located on Fourth Street near Third Avenue. On Fifth Street was the City Planing Mill and Sam Scott, a barber. The Balgay House, for boarders, was located, on Sixth Street. There were many stonecutters living in the Eau Claire area, and there were many employees of the Eau Claire Lumber Company.

Besides Peter Prince there were two John Prince residents in the area.

By 1911 there were ten boarding houses within or in close proximity to the Eau Claire district. The Sun Loy Restaurant was located at 120 Fourth Street West.

In 1912 the Herald Western Printing Company opened a two story brick plant on Sixth Street and Second Avenue.

In 1922 the Normal School was renamed McDougall School and became part of Calgary's Public School System.

In 1935 there were six houses located on Centre Avenue. Eau Claire Avenue had 13 houses located west of the log pond land, and on the east side there were 12 houses. The Central Community Club was located at 514 Eau Claire Avenue.

There were 74 houses on First Avenue, including the Triangle House on the very west end. Commerce included:

The Eau Claire Sawmills, the Dominion Cartage barn (619) Deluxe Auto Body (140) and the backsides of

Western Printers and the Alberta Laundry (700 block) Second Avenue contained at least 119 houses. The Thorpe House, located at 508, was later moved to Heritage Park. The Chinese Mission Y.M.C.A. and the Chinese Public School were located in the 100 block. One block further west was Jack Lyall's grocery and Black and Murray blacksmiths.

The Producers Milk Company occupied a large brick building at 602 Third Avenue. The milk wagons were kept in an adjacent courtyard and its stables and butter department were on First Avenue. Also on Third Avenue were: Ontario Grocery, Lintick's Meat Market, Central Creamery, Central Creamery Confectionary, Blue Label Bottling, Davidson's Confectionary, Summerville's Shoe Repair, Precision Machinery, Hudson's Bay garage and Yee Hing Laundry. The Alberta Laundry, the Western Printing Building, with numerous small offices upstairs, a wagon yard for the milk company and Trotter and Morton Plumbing were business firms on Second Avenue. Adams' Grocery was located on Fifth Street, the Puffed Wheat factory on Sixth Street and Hooving's tire retread plant on Eau Claire Avenue. The sawmill was in its 54th year of operation.

The bridge located just west of 6 A Street, that spanned the log channel, had disappeared, however the timbers on each side of the channel were still in place.

Most of the log pond, located north of First Avenue between Fifth and Sixth Streets, was now filled in, and, except for the swings and slide area on the north side, there was a good crop of alfalfa. The city had developed another small playground on the vacant field on First Avenue east of the laundry.

In 1940 the Canadian Navy constructed a parade square on the old log pond land. The Naval Barracks was located on Seventh Avenue, just east of Third Street West.

Some months later the Calgary Brewing and Malting took over this land and Buffalo Stadium was constructed. This was Calgary's baseball centre, and in the winter there were three lit hockey rinks.

After The War

Following the war Calgary's growth brought about many changes to the Eau Claire as commerce moved in and land and development economics brought about the removal of many houses and some of the older businesses. Fortunately the Prince house, the Thorpe house and a period house on Third Avenue were spared and later moved to Heritage Park. Trotter and Morton, a plumbing firm that had operated in the Eau Claire since 1927, moved out. The Producer's Dairy closed its operations. Brasso Motors opened a car lot on Third Avenue and Centre Street. In 1947 Eric's Used Cars opened on the corner of Seventh Street and Fourth.

The Crystal Skating Rink and Swimming Pool was no more.

By 1959 the Caravan Auto Court was in operation at a location on Fourth Avenue and Fourth Street. By 1964 the historic Braemar Lodge had been pulled down. By 1964 Western International's Calgary Inn was opened and further east on Fourth Avenue the Summit Hotel was now in operation.

In the early 1960's there was pressure to develop the C.P.R. lands and run the railroad tracks along the river.

1961 brought about plans for a residential.-commercial development known as 'Place d'Eau Claire'. In January of 1966 Mayor Jack Leslie announced that a 40 million dollar commercial and residential development is "ready to go".

By 1969 renewal plans for the Eau Claire were in jeopardy as the Hellynea Task Force place emphasis on rehabilitation rather than razing random neighborhoods.

In 1967 the City developed a master plan for future development of Princes Island. The log channel was improved to form a lagoon, with the waste materials added to the low east end of the island, which created about 15 acres of useable land on which native vegetation was planted. Another bridge, a promenade and more walking and bicycle trails were added to the island. The River Café was opened on the island in 1991 and improved on in 1995.

In 1973 the planning department suggested a maximum height of 100 feet for development, but Rod Sykes felt that 50-60 feet should be the maximum. The following year guidelines for Eau Claire development approved by city council restricted the height to three stories within 250 feet of the river, then rising gradually along a 30 degree incline angle. Two of the Eau Claire Estates high rises contravened these guidelines.

In 1976 city arts groups were eyeing Eau Claire land for their planned 125 million dollar arts centre. Later in the year eviction notices were sent out to occupants of many houses on Third Avenue.

In 1979 city council voted for a $250 million development plan for the area. Nu-West sold its interest in the Eau Claire Estates. The large and formerly elegant Connaught Apartments on Fourth Avenue were pulled down.

New planning saw Centre Avenue disappear. Eau Claire Avenue was removed, but the name was given to a new avenue between Fourth and Sixth Streets. First Avenue disappeared west of Seventh Street and east of Sixth Street.

Riverfront Avenue replaced First Avenue east of Second Street. Second Avenue was interrupted at First Street.

The water and brush — 'mud puddle area' that stretch of land between Fourth and Sixth Streets was filled in to diminish the natural area along the Bow.

When James Short School, located just across the street from the Eau Claire district, was demolished in 1969 the copula was saved, put in storage, then moved to Prince's Island. Public donation was paid to have it refurbished and placed on a pedestal. It was officially installed on Canada Day, 1974. Later a new city park was created on part of the old school grounds and the copula was returned to there in 1986.

The 'old Eau Claire' was disappearing. The log channel down steam from Louise Bridge was filled in from excavation material from the downtown area. The sawmill and its old bridge were gone. Buffalo Stadium, the Alberta Laundry, the dairy, residences, rooming houses, the elegant Connaught Apartments, old stables, chicken coops, groceries and corner confectionaries and the Crystal Skating rink were leveled, much of the land to be used as parking lots.

The Transit bus barns and the Greyhound offices moved away. In the parking lots were trees planted by residents many years before.

When 711 Eau Claire Avenue was to be demolished the front door and carved wooden staircase banister were saved to be moved to a newer residence, along with many memories.

In 1980 construction on the Eau Claire Estates was begun. In June 20 interested community associations convinced the Appeal Board that the planned nine 25 story buildings were too high for the location. A 50-story Dome Tower was proposed.

By 1981 plans were made to sell the 4.5 acre barn land for an amount of over ten million dollars. The 162 Eau Claire Estates units were priced from $135,000 to $865,000.

This was the beginning of a ten square block project, but a two year economic recession dampened that.

By the dawn of the 21st Century, a hundred and fourteen years after the sawmill opened and some of its employees built homes in the area, there were still several old residences, a church, the mill office and a commercial building left, but now dwarfed by office and residential towers, the Y.M.C.A. hotels, the Eau Claire Market and numerous parking lots. The Bow River, in all its beauty, flows right along.

A Depiction of Eau Claire Kids Lives

A Cold and

Frosty

Morning

The First

Sliding

The
Vacant Lot

Marbles

Recess
– and
"Crack
the Whip"

Electing
the
Football
Captain

Cartoons by Briggs - The Days of Real Sport

Eau Claire Pictures

10th Street Bridge, log boom

Log Run

Sawdust Burning on Prince's Island   1940's

Eau Claire Mill, Centre Street Bridge   1910

Buffalo Stadium - top left   1950's

View of Log Run on Bow River

Centre Street Bridge, lumber piles 1910

The Eau Claire District 1920's

Aerial View of Eau Claire and the Log Pond....1920's